The Public Confession
of
Johannes Bugenhagen of Pomerania

Concerning the Sacrament of the Body and Blood of Christ

The Public Confession

of

Johannes Bugenhagen of Pomerania

Concerning the Sacrament of the Body and Blood of Christ

On the Basis of the Institution of Christ by which he Renders an Account of his Faith Concerning the Lord's Supper and Says: "Farewell" to those Unwilling to Hear

Mat. 10:29: "There is nothing concealed which will not be revealed, etc."

Isa. 40:8: "The Word of the Lord will endure forever."

As translated by the Rev. Dr. Richard J. Dinda, Prof. Em.

Repristination Press
Malone, Texas

A translation of Johannes Bugenhagen's, *Ioannis Bvgenhagii Pomerani publica, de Sacramento corporis et sanguinis Christi, ex Christi institutione, confeßio: qua suae fidei de coena Domini reddit rationem, Et dicit vale ijs, qui audire nolunt (1528).* Copyright 2015 by Richard Dinda. Published by permission of the translator. No part of this publication may be reproduced, stored in a retrieval system, or transmitted in any form or by any means, electronic, mechanical, photocopying or otherwise without the prior written permission of Repristination Press.

Published in 2015.

REPRISTINATION PRESS
P.O. BOX 173
BYNUM, TEXAS 76631

www.repristinationpress.com

ISBN 1-891469-70-3

Table of Contents

6

Foreword.

It is a great privilege and pleasure to offer a brief word of intro-
duction to Dr. Richard Dinda's translation of *Ioannis Bvgenhagii
Pomerani publica, de Sacramento corporis et sanguinis Christi, ex Christi institutione, confeßio: qua suae fidei de coena Domini reddit rationem, Et dicit
vale ijs, qui audire nolunt* (1528). Dr. Dinda's translation is particularly
helpful to the Church because it presents Bugenhagen's argument
in its entirety, with his concerns regarding the corrupted edition of
his annotations on the Psalms set in the broader context of other
statements which he had made regarding the Lord's Supper, and
clearly setting forth the distinction between the biblical teaching
regarding the Sacrament of the Altar and the corrupt teachings of
'Sacramentarians' and Papists alike.

Bugenhagen's experience of having Martin Bucer publish a
corrupted edition of his *Psaltery* is hardly an isolated experience in
the Church; false teachers hidden within the Church love to twist
the writings of the Orthodox to conform to their 'new teaching.' As
Bugenhagen demonstrates, what the 'Sacramentarians' did to him
they also did to the writings of the ancient church fathers, as the
'Sacramentarians' shamelessly endeavored to read their false teachings back into church fathers. For those of us who have encountered
the difficulties of counteracting the efforts of nineteenth and twen-
tieth century 'Lutherans' to read their new doctrines back into the
Age of Lutheran Orthodoxy and the early church, the 'Sacramentarian' tactic is quite familiar.

Repristination Press was started for the simple purpose of
allowing modern Lutherans to read the fathers of the Confessional
Era and Age of Orthodoxy without experiencing the 'filtering' im-

posed by certain Lutherans of previous generations. After twenty-two years of publishing such works, we remain confident that the way for modern Lutherans to encounter the Lutheran fathers is to let those great teachers speak for themselves, and to ignore those who want to tell us that what they 'actually' meant was the opposite of what they wrote. As becomes clear throughout Bugenhagen's *Public Confession*, the fathers had very little patience for such nonsense.

+*James D. Heiser, M.Div., S.T.M.*
Bishop, the Evangelical Lutheran Diocese of North America
Publisher, Repristination Press

Johannes Bugenhagen
To Johannes Brenz,
preacher of the sacred Gospel of Christ
at Halle, Schwabia:

Grace and peace from God, our Father, and from our Lord, Jesus Christ.

Honorable Johannes:

The things which I have written to all I have been unwilling to publish without your name that all may know that I both love and respect the name of him who for a long time already has been making known and publishing to the world many erudite and godly writings on behalf of the Word of God for the salvation of many. Keep on, and may the Lord be with you. Amen.

Here again I am repeating the reason for my faith regarding the Lord's Supper against the Sacramentarian deniers. I was compelled to do this not only because of my office but also that my Gospel not become suspect to good people after my interpreter in the German Psaltery made me a Sacramentarian before the whole world with his public writings and teaching, although I was crying out against him. Some Anabaptists are saying that there was some book from Nitelspurg under my name, which book was filled with Sacramentarian blasphemies. This obviously was an egregious work of men who assert with their lies and false charges things which they want to teach as the truth of God.

We know, honorable Brenz, that some people for this reason have wanted us not to contend against others as if the matter were not of such importance, but as if we should hold it in contempt when we see that some are denying the word of Christ and are establishing the human word as its substitute. Rather, let us be as careful as possible of the snares of Satan when he touches those external things which the institution of Christ has consecrated and given to us. You see, Satan is acting as if this Sacrament is an unnecessary thing and as if the Gospel and everything else can stand firm without those external items.

We are not unaware that the pope has taken from us the entire Gospel of communion by his "one kind," as they call it, as if to commune in this way is necessary and useful to the laity, while they are neglecting the institution of Christ and thus are holding it in contempt. In so doing, they have restored very many abominations of their Masses into the place of the blood of Christ which they have forbidden to the laity. So also now, when some Sacramentarians see that the truth is pressing them hard, they want to appear to be considering a peaceful solution and thus to be settling the matter. They say: "Grant that a person is a Christian, and he will receive in the Supper also the physical body of Christ. Let nothing else come to the bread, etc." We must not agree with just any appearance of the bread, for this is not our cause but the cause of God.

In addition to the things we see, we are not seeing what evils are going to come from their taking away the Gospel. To be sure, Satan has revealed himself for a great part, for he is battling against the clear word of Christ, whose betrayers we ought to be through no charity.

I therefore wanted to set forth those few points which I had already offered for a long time ahead of the others which follow that I might confound those who declare publicly that I either did feel then or now feel in favor of the Sacramentarians contrary to the institution of Christ.

Next, I confess in detail what I feel about what they call "consecration," that is, from which it happens that the bread of the Lord becomes His body and the cup His blood. Among these things, I am also treating all the words which have been written about this institution of Christ. After this, I am writing against some unique type of Sacramentarians and what I feel about the very sacred discourse of Christ written in John 6. Deniers of the word of Christ should not expect from me other things after those [i.e., that have been written]. Let them fear Christ, whom they assail in His Word. I am sure they will not overcome Him.

You, then, my beloved friend Johannes, read my words, of whatever value they may be. I am in the habit of reading your words, and I love them. Farewell. Also, see to it that you and other pastors publicly admonish your people to invoke the mercy of our Father endlessly that Satan would be trampled beneath our feet as soon as possible. I know what I am wishing, and I have no doubt but that you are always doing that which you are in the habit of admonishing diligently in your writings.

Again, farewell. Sent from Wittenberg on the Thursday after Jubilate, 1528.

Johannes Bugenhagen of Pomerania
to the very learned Dr. Hess,
pastor of the Church in Bratislava:

The grace of God through Christ be yours! I do not have anything to write at this time, most learned doctor, if we do not wish here success for the Gospel of the glory of God through Christ with all the honor which we also owe our enemies. For, what would I write when Dr. Maiobanus[1], who will be our mouth and letter, returns to you? Furthermore, the same doctor asked me to write a few words to you as to what I think we should respond to the new errors which have developed regarding the Sacrament of the Eucharist. You will respond no more certainly than from the actual grammar of Scripture—which those masters of error tear to pieces wretchedly. Although you may not need them, I serve you with these few words, now that I have been asked.

"This [hoc] is My body; this [hic] is My blood." It is contrary to the use of speaking every language that the demonstrative pronoun demonstrate something in this passage other than that which it strives to point out. This error of Carlstadt displeases even Zwingli, namely in the pronouns "hic" and "hoc."[2]

Furthermore, because Zwingli does not see well that the matter has yielded in the pronoun "this," he takes the verb "is" and contends that it is taken not substantively but significatively, citing examples where it is taken in this way. However, Christ is not explaining here some dream or parable. Also, when the three evan-

1 Ambrosius Maiobanus (1494–1554), reformer of Breslau.
2 Translator note: "Hoc," the neuter form, points to the neuter "corpus - body"; the masculine "hic," to the masculine "sanguis - blood."

gelists and Paul wrote about this subject, not a single one indicated with so much as a word that "is" is taken significatively. Therefore, they are obviously saying something different, as I shall quickly point out.

However, because he sees that we immediately have a *non sequitur*, namely, that if "is" elsewhere is taken for "signifies," therefore it is taken here for "signifies"; otherwise, wherever it would be taken for "signifies," as, for instance: "Man is a living creature," that is: "'Man' signifies a living creature." It therefore remains that he prove that "this" here is taken in this way. Nevertheless he has nothing else to dream about so strongly than this: "The flesh does not produce anything." Here we laugh at that great theologian along with his friend Carlstadt. "This" and "is" just lie there.

Who does not see that there Christ is condemning the carnal understanding of the disciples? When He opposes "flesh" to "spirit," He is no longer speaking about His own flesh and blood as before, but about flesh and the spirit, just as Scripture everywhere condemns the flesh and approves of the spirit and that it never calls flesh "the letter." "All flesh is grass," [1 Peter 1:25] "The judgment of the flesh is death, etc." However, Peter says: "You have the words of eternal life."

Christ is not saying here: "My flesh is of no benefit"; otherwise, He would be making Himself a liar, for He had said: "My flesh is for the life of the world." You may have said that it is of no benefit to you to know from what source the life of the world comes. Or is the life of the world, which was dead and damned before, nothing?

Furthermore, Christ says simply: "The flesh is of no benefit," [John 6:63] just as He said elsewhere to Peter: "Flesh and blood have not revealed this to you, but My Father," that is, the Spirit of God, etc. No flesh is beneficial except that in which God is, for "the Word became flesh," [John 1:14]; just as no water is beneficial except the water of Baptism in which the Word of God is present.

14

Also, no bread is beneficial, but that bread is beneficial in which the body of Christ is, because of the word of Christ which cannot lie. Those words: "The flesh is of no benefit, etc." condemn all wisdom, righteousness, and whatever belongs to men, but they do want us to be "God-taught."

Therefore it would have been wicked to relate this to that flesh in which God is present, by which flesh we have been sanctified. Therefore, you see that Zwingli has nothing and that he is not a theologian here. That he calls us the "devourers of Christ and eaters of His flesh" is blasphemy, for we are not tearing at the flesh of Christ but are eating bread and, in the bread, the body of Christ which we neither see nor chew with our teeth. We believe that He is present and that we are eating Him because of the words of Christ.

SEE THE GRAMMAR FROM PAUL.

"The cup of blessing which we bless (more commonly "which we consecrate"), is it not the communion of the blood of Christ?" [1 Cor. 10:16] That is, it is the sharing by which the blood of Christ is shared and distributed to you, to me, and to others so that that very treasure is being distributed and becomes common to us.

"The bread which we break, is it not the communion of the body of Christ?," [ibid.] namely, that by which the body of Christ is communicated to us, etc. Therefore, the body and blood of Christ are truly present there. He says: "That bread which we break and that cup which we consecrate, etc."

He is indeed signifying a spiritual union when he says: "We who are many are one bread and one body," but he adds: "…because we all are partaking of the one bread." [1 Cor. 10:17] He is saying: "We are one among ourselves because of the one bread which we are eating." But how is there one bread which you are eating in Bratislava and we are eating in Wittenberg, unless that be the one body of Christ? After all, there is no doubt but that Paul is speaking about external bread.

He took bread, broke it, and said: "Take; eat; this is My body which is broken for you (that is, for your benefit)," and He distributed it to each, just as we read: "Break your bread for him who is hungry," that is, break it and distribute it. He is blind who doesn't see that the body of Christ is in the bread, that all who receive it take the whole body of Christ, and that only the bread is broken externally. Because it is the body of Christ, the body of Christ is also broken, that is, it is distributed to many people, and yet no part of the body of Christ is given to individuals as part bread but as the [whole] body of Christ. You see, these words come first: "He took bread and broke it," just as Paul had said earlier: "The bread which we break..." He also adds: "This is My body which is broken for you." The body of Christ is present, but what is it to me *how* it is here? He who has instituted it will have seen to it, provided I believe this and do that which He has committed to me.

This cup is the new testament. Go through all Scripture, and you will not discover another thing called "the new testament" and the remission of sins [8] through Christ or through the blood of Christ, as Jeremiah writes about the new testament: "I shall remember their sins no more" [31:34]. If, then, this cup is the new testament, there certainly is a forgiveness of sins which people wickedly attribute to the wine. Therefore, the blood of Christ is in the wine. This is something which they should explain when we read the additional: "...in My blood," as we read in the evangelists, "which is shed for the remission of sins."

Paul says: "...he will be guilty of the body and blood of the Lord"; but he does not say: "He will be guilty of the bread and wine."

"...[N]ot discerning the body of the Lord." Those certainly do not recognize the body of the Lord who say that this is simple bread, and also when they do not recognize those who believe that the body of Christ is present there but do not grasp how Christ is united with the bread so that they eat in remembrance of Him, etc.

Tell me, please, in these two passages in which he has no evidence allowing him to say so, how will Zwingli say: "'Is' is taken as 'signifies'"? The text reads: "He will be guilty of the body and blood of the Lord, for he does not discern the body of the Lord." Paul does not say: "He will be guilty of the signified body and blood of the Lord," but of His true body and blood, present as they are in the bread and wine. Paul here is speaking about the person who eats and drinks and does not say: "...not recognizing the signified body of the Lord, etc."

Well, I have shown you the forest.
But, farewell in Christ, and pray God the Father on behalf of us.

In this letter, regardless of the variety of the things which I have attacked, I do not yet see anything for which I am sorry. Zwingli wants me to have spoken incorrectly. This is a new error. If you look back on that which some people have felt, said, and written against the institution of Christ, this is not a new error. No Sacramentarian church, that is, no church which denies this institution of Christ, has ever been established[3], as now several of them are being established, regardless of how some people once howled against the churches of Christ. Give me an example of even one church from the time of the apostles which has observed and taught publicly the way the Sacramentarians are doing today.

For this reason, I have said that this a new error. Otherwise, tell me one article of faith against which some people have not spoken. Next, he [Zwingli] will laugh at me for mentioning the consecration, but later you will see my statement based on the word of Christ. Moreover, that I may forget the consecration or blessing, he tries to persuade me that we must read in Paul: "The cup of blessing

---

3 In other words, no such sectarian church existed in the days of the early church.

which we bless" is something which I am offering to the learned for their laughter, unless they should have wanted to allow us to read: "The bread which we break…"

JOHANNES BUGENHAGEN OF POMERANIA
sends greetings to
THE VERY LEARNED GENTLEMEN
GEORGE SPALATIN, PASTOR OF THE
CHURCH IN ALDENBURG,
and
JOHANNES AGRICOLA, HEADMASTER OF
THE SCHOOL OF EISLEBEN,
who are now living in Speyer
and who are his teachers and brothers.

My beloved brothers in Christ, you will certainly grieve over my misfortune when you will have seen my prayer. What do you think is going to happen on account of our corrupters after we have died, when they have corrupted our books so much while we are still living? However, God shall have seen to those matters. Because you are now in that place where people perhaps are purchasing and reading that German psaltery which has been published under my name and where some people are intimating that I have the same feelings as those Sacramentarians; I say, because of all that, I am sending you the very Pomeranian to speak for himself, that he in the meantime might be permitted to be of concern to you. You see, although you are my best patrons in this case; nevertheless, because you are my Pomeranian brothers, may people now believe that you are speaking on my behalf in this hateful case. The Lord be with you.

JOHANNES BUGENHAGEN OF POMERANIA ON HIS PSALTERY TRANSLATED INTO GERMAN AND PUBLISHED IN BASEL IN 1526 A.D.

My commentaries which I had written in Latin on the psaltery of David have been translated into German in Strasbourg by Martin Bucer. This year they have been published in German for the first time from the printing house of Adam Petrus of the city of Basel. In the pages thereof, there are several statements which are not up to my standards, but I tolerate them easily, for I rejoice that ultimately Christ is preached in any way at all.

However, I shall not tolerate those opinions that have been mixed in with my statements under my name. Indeed, I cannot but judge them as wicked (May Christ love me for this!). These occur in the commentary on Psa. 110 which begins in this way: "I shall confess to you, etc." Those statements were inserted about the Eucharist, as if I am a defender of that opinion which denies that the faithful—contrary to the clear words of Christ's institution—eat the true body of Christ and drink His true blood in the Eucharist. This is as if we must fight against the word of Christ in the same way as we have been battling human traditions and the wicked abuse of this very sacred Sacrament.

But I am asking[4] whether I am not he who has borne witness of his own opinion not only in other books but also in public in a letter to Dr. Hess against this opinion? I did this in such a way that I provoked the Sacramentarians to publish pamphlets against

---

4 Text reads "*Quasi*," but it reads better as "*Quaeso*."

me, which abused me, some with their erudition but others with their most inappropriate ineptitudes, and these not so much against me as against the word of Christ. What interpreter of mine could ignore those? With what conscience did he dare to impose upon the world the idea that I felt and taught in such a way? Would I tell here these censures, were I to deal with that treachery with dignified words? Well, as the world has judged, these are not censures but the truth.

However, I am doing this neither to defend my name nor to efface the name of anyone else. Let God take care of that. In His just judgment, He wants those who have not taken up a love for the truth to be misled by lies. I am now doing this only that I not allow things which I do not feel, and therefore what is contrary to what I feel about the institution of Christ, to be published under my name. Or I am doing this that, if there are some people who enjoy being misled and following human thoughts, they not say (contrary to my public testimonies) that I am either the instigator of, or cooperator in, their seduction.

You see, I am so far from wishing Bucer evil that I even grieve that he has fallen into these difficulties and that I must now say with sorrow what I have to say after that opinion was published not only under my name but also in that outstanding work of the Psalms, unless I should wish to have a partner in misleading by keeping silent. He himself is my witness as to the valuation I made the man and with what frankness I esteemed him so that I entrusted my *Psaltery* to his judgment. In that preface of his in the *Psaltery* he writes that I wrote to him in this way, and truly I do write this now.

"My friend Bucer, interpret this *Psaltery* of mine as freely as you wish. Change it, add to it, take away from it, place things in a different order, interpret some matters more clearly or in a different way so that it is no longer my, but rather your, *Psaltery*. Here I shall allow you all these things for which on my advice you may have hoped for our Germans that those who now are unlearned children may learn something of the psalms in the understanding of which shortly before its publication even the most learned professors merely talked idly. Have at it, then, and may the Lord be with you! Amen."

These are my words, just as Bucer himself truly is writing, to which he adds the following: "These are the words of my interpreter, Johannes of Pomerania, and he has written them to me in his own handwriting, according to which I have restrained myself so far that I have inserted none of those matters which the Pomeranian himself had written usefully in Latin for the true and genuine understanding of the psalms, although I had redacted them into a different order which seemed more practical for laymen." So much for him.

If he has provided that which he promised, I rejoice, for I have not seen everything. But, tell me please, from what source did that Sacramentarian cause creep into my *Psaltery?* Perhaps this book appeared to be appropriate, for in it are all the things which they feel against us or which reveal our resistance to them and which they are peddling under our name. Who doesn't know that this is the sort of thing that is happening?

Let it be a matter of conscience that he was unwilling to defend our opinion about the Eucharist even by giving an account of it or by interpreting it. Why didn't he omit it totally, when he himself correctly asserts that it is not necessary to speak about the Sacrament of the Eucharist in this psalm? I certainly would have praised him as a good man who, because of conscience, did not dare report to the Germans my errors (as he himself wishes to appear to be doing). After all, we are not demanding of him that he act or speak or err in one way or another against his conscience. Why did he seek, where there was no need, an opportunity for inserting his own dogma as if it were mine that he might in this way contaminate my name and ministry of the Word, which God had entrusted to me? Why did he make me suspect to the faithful while, in the meantime, I was feeling only the best things about him?

However, every excuse will be ridiculous here, for I have spoken here only a few words about the Sacrament. These words say nothing about that new opinion which he himself with a good conscience (as all Sacramentarians witness) could not only have given word for word, but also could have preached publicly. Moreover, on account of these words I do not feel that what my opinion is teaching, I have given witness in clear language in the preceding psalm: "The Lord has said, etc." Thus, let me not say that, when I was writing, I wasn't even permitted to suspect that this fire against the institution of Christ would at some time ensue.

Perhaps however, the same words of mine by which I made it free for him to add to, take away from, etc. my words, not only will excuse him but even charge me with acting unjustly in accusing him because of that addition, as if I may not have prescribed to him the statements which contain it, or for the obvious reason that he published under my name statements which he did not know we publicly condemned. Also, someone else could have added to my statements the following and similar statements, such as: "The bread is a stone"; "Water is fire"; "A Turk is a Christian"; "God is not in control, etc." Then later, he could be excused and therefore contend that he had acted correctly, because I had permitted him to add what he wished, obviously, that he might provide what I thereby had hoped for.

Other people should see here my candor. Moreover, I clearly am accusing my foolishness; in fact, I am admitting that I am a sinner because I committed to the judgment of a human that treasury of the Word of God which God had entrusted to me. This I did, despite the fact that I myself teach that we must trust no one save the one God, however much charity is the servant of all. I must be absolutely foolish if I not act more cautiously after this in those matters of faith. You see, with this foolishness of mine (to confess naively) I have rendered suspect not so much myself as all the finest people and those who are men in our consideration and who by the grace of God are most deserving of the Gospel of Christ, as if they feel the same about the Eucharist as I do. However, no one of us who teach publicly feels this way, although we may easily alleviate that plague without suspicion. Now let me explain the way in which this happened.

When I had scarcely begun to explain the elegance of the German *Psaltery*, I began to act cheerfully, as if I had taken correct care of all the things with which I wanted to deal. But then, after nearly half a year, someone came from Augsburg and indicated that that Sacramentarian opinion had been inserted into the *Psaltery*. At first, I was shocked. Then, when he had added: "Because you are said to have written in such a way, people are saying that the whole school of Wittenberg therefore feels the same way," I began to laugh, thinking that the fellow was absurd.

I said: "What does it have to do with the whole school if one Pomeranian felt and wrote in this way?" When I pondered the matter more deeply, I observed that this report was not absolutely inane and that here that father of lies, Satan, had a sufficiently appropriate appearance and grace to persuade people that we all feel that way.

That preface of mine is addressed to the very illustrious Prince Frederick, elector of Saxony, the memory of whom is blessed, and was placed at the front of the *Psaltery*. In this preface, I admit that in our school I have taught those things which I am writing in the *Psaltery*. Furthermore, I have added the commendations of Doctor Martin Luther and of Philip Melanchthon, by which I commend to the reader all the things which I have written in the *Psaltery*.

Therefore, when people read in the German *Psaltery* a wicked opinion about the Sacrament, they will say that the Pomeranian

not only felt this way, but also asserted this publicly in our school
as confirmed by the public testimony of Doctor Martin and Philip
when the Pomeranian asserted publicly that he taught it in school.
They will say: "Those two eminent men confirm whatever the Pomeranian wrote in his *Psaltery*. The whole school, therefore, in this
area not only does not speak up against the Pomeranian but even
teaches the same thing as he does." That is what Satan wanted. People say that those things are printed in the Latin and are being sent
to the French and to those who don't know German. If those subjects deal with the business of God, why do we need those begged
and fabricated supports?

I therefore implore you, Christian reader, that with both
words and letters you warn your people whom these words of ours
perhaps are not reaching. Advise them, if they should happen upon
that German *Psaltery*, that they not take up under our name this
opinion about the Sacrament which denies that the faithful eat the
true body of Christ when they eat the bread of Christ and that they
are drinking the true blood of Christ when they drink the cup of
Christ. After all, even if their opinion were true, advise them that
the Pomeranian feels and teaches publicly in this school just as he
wrote to the very illustrious Prince Frederick of Saxony and just as
those men, Dr. Martin and Philip, confirmed this opinion of the
Pomeranian with a public commendation. This is so wicked that,
even if I were to remain silent (O that I had been allowed to remain
silent!), as many people as have heard and read our words, even if
they be our foes, are compelled to cry out that this is such a shameful lie that nothing could be said more shamefully.

I am unwilling to be an associate of those who keep upsetting good consciences for the deliverance of which Christ died, and
who are delaying the course of the Gospel that some may be offended by that disagreement but others carry on nothing other than
Sacramentarian business, as if revealing the Gospel is nothing, as if

the forgiveness of sins is nothing, as if consciences which faith has pacified are nothing, as if it is nothing that we acknowledge that we have become the children of God, as if it is nothing that the correct use of the Sacraments has been indicated to the world. Although they are able to upset consciences, they are unable to comfort any consciences, not even their own nor those who appear to be the more sane among them, nor can they render that conscience certain about their own figurative use of "is" which they have invented. As witnesses against them, there are very many books which they themselves have published about this opinion. The person who does not require that certainty in their books is worthy of reading nothing other than such writings.

I said that I am unwilling to be an associate of those people so that I fall away from the sure words of Christ (who does not deceive me) into the dubious interpretations of human beings. I know that, according to the admonition of the apostle Peter, the person who speaks (that is, who has the office of teaching) must be certain that he is speaking nothing but the discourses of God, and I am fully aware of that statement of Paul: "He who disturbs you will bear the judgment, regardless of who he may have been." [Gal. 5:10]

I am surprised, however, that, wishing as they do to find the gatekeepers asleep, they say that all the ancients from the time of the apostles both felt and wrote in favor of this Sacramentarian opinion. Perhaps they hope that there is no one except their very own selves who either may have seen or may intend to use the writings of the ancients. Tell me, please, with what conscience do they dare to assert such things who nevertheless boast in their published writings that they have examined very closely all the things which the ancients have written?

The ancients indeed have written many things about the spiritual eating and the use of the Christian Eucharist just as we have been doing up to this point with our preaching and writing.

Those who have been instructed by the appropriate passages and words from the institution of Christ confess with Christ in clear words that the bread and cup of the Lord (which we say is the Eucharist) is the true—and not the false—body and blood of the Lord which the disciples ate.

Furthermore, I call "disciples of Christ" those who, instructed through the Gospel, confess (or appear to confess) Christ and those things which are of Christ, regardless of what sort of people they may appear to be before God, who alone knows how to differentiate true disciples from false ones when they are hiding. After all, at the end of the age, first all the offenses and workers of unfaithfulness will be gathered out of this kingdom of Christ. This you will see quite clearly in those ancients. Furthermore, the ancients write fearlessly about the Eucharist so that they don't even appear to be suspect, although posterity may feel something other than that the body and blood of Christ are present in the Eucharist. In fact, the most elegant post-apostolic writer, Tertullian, whom (just as others) these people use to abuse us, asserts our opinion in his book on the resurrection of the flesh and says: "Our flesh eats the body and blood of Christ so that the soul, too, is nourished by God." What could one say more clearly? Take a look at that passage there that you may see that where Tertullian elsewhere says "the figure of the body," that figure is not the figure of Tertullian which they are inventing for themselves. Therefore, it is just as true that the ancients denied that the body and blood of the Lord are present in the Eucharist as it is that the school of Wittenberg teaches that [denial].

It is not the business of this effort to deal with its actual cause. Let him who believes me believe. Let him who argues with me argue. Furthermore, through the things which I have been saying so far, I want very much that that which is very well-known become known to all, to wit, that this is not my statement about the Eucharist which is read as if it were ours in that German *Psaltery* about which we have been speaking. God knows that I have spoken according to my conscience. I readily forgive all, provided they stop disturbing consciences which their opinion cannot comfort.

In addition, with reference to the Latin *Psaltery* which was first published in 1524, I assure both buyers and sellers that they not be afraid that later I want to make that former [German translation] better, and that they not believe the printers who are always adding or correcting something which has been emended and again corrected, etc. As I have made clear from the beginning, so much as it is in my power, I pray that my Latin *Psaltery* should continue to be a reminder of that outstanding gift of God by which He granted me the strength to force myself through to the end of the Psalms without another guide, when my daily lectures were urging me daily [to find another].

Furthermore, I am not arrogating so much for myself that I desire to indicate to others in this light of the Gospel all things which require either another or a clearer interpretation in my *Psaltery*, as if others may see nothing, and as if an opportunity has been given to someone who is not wise enough to understand, especially at this time when Dr. Martin [Luther] has made the *Psaltery* in the German language so clear that one can use it even in place of a commentary.

If there were no other reason, nevertheless I am unwilling to change anything for the sake of those who want to be schoolmasters in someone else's book when they are permitted to find something with which to respond. To these I am unwilling to yield, but I want to leave it free to each person to pass judgment about the meaning of the Psalms. In fact, why are they not translating one of the prophets whom we have not yet translated during our times that we may see their command thereof? Let them read my preface, and they will see in my *Psaltery* that through Christ I have accomplished what I had promised. I know that I have scant stuff, but God has given me the mind to be able to restrain myself within my limits.

Later, perhaps, printers will exhibit my *Psaltery* printed more clearly and with greater care, but they will not exhibit one which I shall have enlarged. If, however, it may have seemed best at some time that I add something, I shall do this separately by publishing a booklet lest I burden people who bought our first edition with another purchase. I have spoken.

As I see, after my public accusation my friend Bucer is excusing me in a public writing in such a way that he is wiping his mouth as if he committed no sin against me, but he does that in vain. You see, he wants it to appear as if he has spoken nothing against either me or the institution of Christ with his Sacramentarian addition to my *Psaltery*. These are his words among the rest which he writes there about his own Sacrament.

He says: "As Christ handed the bread to His disciples, He said: 'This is My body'; but He commanded them to eat it and sent them back to His own body which kept being given over into death for them that they might believe that this was His body, that they might receive it internally and that they might eat it spiritually, because what is corporal is not beneficial and, in fact, rather gets in the way of being a blessing. He therefore wanted them to believe just as He physically gave them the bread and wine to take up; in this way, He would be giving them His body and blood for a divine life in the fact that He was handing them (His body and blood) over into death on their behalf. He wanted them to believe that they had to eat spiritually that which alone leads to eternal life, just as the Lord teaches clearly in John 6."

These words of Bucer (not to mention other passages) you read in the German *Psaltery* as my words, by which he obviously is denying that the bread about which Christ says: "This is My body" is the body of Christ, and that the cup about which Christ says: "This is My blood" is the blood of Christ. He also says that, it is a hindrance if anything corporal is present there. I would tell what sort of things these are and what they don't mean and what it means that the words of Christ are spirit and life, and this I would do most truthfully, not through false charges as they are in the habit of sweeping over me, were I to rejoice to write against men and to vindicate myself, something which I am not doing. I presented my meaning in the following book sufficiently, although even before it was necessary that it become perfectly well-known on the basis of my public writings, which they admit they have read.

These are things which Bucer ought not have made public under my name in the *Psaltery*. As I have never felt that way, so also I have never taught nor written in that way. If God shall have permitted it, let them be deceivers under their own name and not under someone else's.

Christ instituted that people eat the bread which He says is His body. Bucer says that Christ ordered people to eat the bread which is not His body. But didn't He who says: "Take, eat, this is My body," command us to eat His body by eating the bread which He certainly says is His body? Or didn't something come to this bread not for the sake of the bread but for our sake when this word of Christ comes to it, provided you who intend to receive this Sacrament believe this word? But I shall speak about these matters later. Bucer, therefore, is speaking in favor of neither my way of thinking nor of the institution of Christ. It is about this that I accuse him before the entire Church.

Furthermore, if anyone wished to know if that of which he is accusing me is true, he should read my speech against him, although what holiness would it be, were I to adorn his wicked dogma with good words? Obviously, no saints have ever done this nor did Christ Himself do this. Correct?

Additionally, he notes my 'arrogance' in that I wrote (after that opinion was published not only under my name but also in my outstanding work of the Psalms, etc.): "It is a work of great skill and of great love to say: 'Your *Psaltery* is not of such great value as you are making it,'" as if I ever magnified my name in my public writings. But now the Latin person doesn't know what this outstanding work means to the Latins. I knew that this was a book which many people wanted for themselves, because it promised some sort of interpretation of the Psalms which would not perish immediately or for the sake of the sacred Psalms themselves when many other futile dialogs and awkward pamphlets (not to say wicked ones) are now being published here and there.

Next, what if I had said that this outstanding work of the Psalms was not my commentaries but those which Bucer had made his own out of mine? I perhaps would not have sinned. He might have been able to take my words in that way, because he was ignorant of my way of thinking, and here charity would have been favorably inclined unless calumny were in charge. Furthermore, is the work of the Psalms outstanding of itself even if my commentaries or those of others aren't available? Therefore this ought not be a case of seeing the speck in a brother's eye.

What negative effect, however, do false charges have upon me when at the end I write about the Latin *Psaltery* things which have nothing to do with favoring my case? How much would I have sinned there, if through Christ I had not been loosed from the man of sin? Or will I not be permitted what Augustine was permitted, namely, to retract some things from my prior books which still remain unharmed, etc? But, if God may have wanted something else, I shall not resist the divine will in order to save my own words.

Let God bring it about that we all say the same thing with one mind and one spirit according to the Word of God and the Gospel of our Lord Jesus Christ. Amen.

On the other hand, when Bucer, Zwingli, and Oecolampadius contend in their public writings that I wrote in [my commentary on] that psalm in favor of their way of thinking and against my own, I shall attribute all my words about which they themselves speak from that passage to this point. Thus I have written.

This is the greatest Sacrament; that is, the Word made flesh. It is nourishment for those who fear God; that is, for believers who acknowledge their sins and who believe that they are refreshed by that bread alone. Those who do not fear God can never eat this Sacrament, as you see clearly those words of John 6. Moreover, eating this Sacrament is to believe that Christ became flesh and blood for your sake and gave up both in the matter of your salvation. If you believe in this way, you have eternal life.

Up to this point, I have been saying nothing about the Sacrament of the Lord's Supper, but I have been speaking about spiritual eating, that is, about the faith by which we always become incorporated in Him so long as we believe Christ. I shall speak later about this faith on the basis of John 6. However, after these words about the Sacrament of the Supper, I add immediately the following: The external Sacrament of the bread and wine or of the body and blood of Christ is so great a sign of this faith that without it you receive the Sacrament unworthily to your own judgment. Therefore I claim that we must never teach or write about the external Sacrament of the Eucharist without that of which we have spoken (namely, that it is indeed taken from our eyes into heaven but nevertheless is always present by its own power to those who fear God), obviously, that we not appear to receive the Sacrament without faith. Up to this point, I have been repeating my words from the *Psaltery*.

First, when I had not yet written these things, the Sacramentarian deniers had not yet appeared; otherwise, fearful as I was of them, I wouldn't have said: "This is only a sign of"; I say, "…of this," namely, that the Word became flesh, and that in this way it was paid out on the cross. If my words should displease anyone, I ask only this: that he cast them out that the words of Christ may remain unharmed for us, whatever you may think of mine. Indeed, I spoke more freely when the matter was outside of contention, just as Augustine, too, at times spoke more freely about the subject because not even at his time did the Church believe anything like this [i.e., the Sacramentarian doctrine]. Nevertheless, with these words I have spoken the truth, and I have asserted nothing in favor of the Sacramentarians.

Inasmuch as I have said twice about the external Sacrament that this is only a sign; when I see it, I say that I am seeing the body of Christ. When I touch it, I am touching the body of Christ; when I eat it, I am eating the body of Christ. Yet, in the meantime, I am seeing bread, I am touching bread, I am eating bread. If you look at the external character of the Sacrament, the senses can pass no other judgment. But faith alone says that, because of the word of Christ, this is the body of Christ, and, as it believes, so it is, for faith does not believe this without the Word of God.

Therefore I was not denying this when I said about the external Sacrament that it contained something within itself, namely, the body and blood of Christ according to the institution of Christ. However, the former, to wit, the external Sacrament, I said was a sign, although what is there, that is, the body and blood of Christ, is not the sign but what has been signed.

If they were not rejoicing to be making false charges, they ought to have seen that this is my way of thinking from my commentaries on the Psalm above, although I said it in a few words. You see, I have always been concerned to inculcate faith in our people that they not approach the Sacrament without faith and without trust in Christ and in this way eat and drink to their judgment. These words of mine, however, which they boast that I wrote them in their favor and which almost all of them have read, as they witness in their public writings, are a witness for us Wittenbergians against their shameless lies with which they misrepresent us to the world as if we be teaching that our sins are forgiven because of the eating of the carnal Sacrament.

FINAL CONFESSION
OF JOHANNES BUGENHAGEN OF POMERANIA
CONCERNING THE CONSECRATION,
as they call it:
that is, from what source are the body and blood of Christ
made for us in the Lord's Supper,
and by what power do we give and receive this Sacrament?

Let our Sacramentarians today cease wondering how it can happen that in the Sacrament we eat the body of Christ and drink His blood, when the body of Christ sits on the right hand of majesty in the heavens, as they in the meantime fear that we are taking Christ away from those thrones. For forty days after His resurrection, Christ revealed His whole self to His disciples. Although He had been glorified in the glory of the Father (something which no one should deny and which we will show from obvious Scripture in our pamphlet entitled *Fragments*), yet in so dense a body that one could touch it and by touch and sight could judge it to have flesh and bones which a spirit does not have. In the meantime, however, He did not abandon His own glory into which He had entered through His death. That same Christ was present physically on earth, and yet He was ruling at the right hand of the Father; —yes, that same Christ who had been killed did not in the meantime leave His throne vacant.

But if Christ had been thrown into some one corner of heaven, and if the right hand of God was the sort of thing which they themselves [the Sacramentarians] imagine, then our human reasoning and understanding are not stupid. In fact, we shall even say that we are speaking the truth.

You see, if we shall have abandoned the Word of God (not to mention all the articles of faith) and admitted the judgment of reason to divine matters, it also seems strange to us (and to whom wouldn't it?) not only how it could happen in the Sacrament that Christ gives His own body and blood to the faithful, who nevertheless are confessing that He ascended into heaven and is not going to return until the last day, but also in the Last Supper, while He was wholly present in His body and blood, He gave to the individual disciples His body and blood without fearing that people might believe He had many bodies so that, if Peter ate His body and James and John did, too, they might think that He lied when He said: "Eat; this is My body" and "Drink; this is My blood," if they saw His whole body still sitting there when they were eating.

However, such wonders or miracles do not turn believers away from the consideration of the Sacrament, as the Sacramentarians imagine, because such miracles do not engross us. We know that they are miracles, and we permit them to remain as miracles. We do not follow the dreams of human reason, nor do those things which God has commanded us overwhelm us. We freely admit that God is wiser than we. Instead, we follow the word of Christ, and for this reason we are absolutely certain of what He instituted, what He said, and what He commanded: that we not be ignorant of that very thing which we call "the Eucharist."

We add nothing to that word [Eucharist] nor do we take anything from it, unlike the papists; for we do not make from it a sacrifice for the living and the dead in order to devour the homes of widows and the courts of rulers and to extol ourselves higher than God. We do not set that apart and reserve it so that the common folk may only worship it but not eat it. We do not carry it about, etc. After all, Christ did not give us this sacrifice for those purposes. We do not forbid the other "kind" (as they call it), or the cup of the Lord, to the laity, because we know that, as Christ instituted the whole Sacrament, He Himself also gave it, and He did not make some difference of His disciples (that is, of Christians) in accepting the Sacrament, just as you see they observed in the Corinthian Church and at the time of the ancient teachers of the Church.

However, we are not corrupting the words of Christ by creating figurative expressions, as do our Sacramentarians, who wretchedly twist themselves and Scripture when they use it to build up bronze walls (as they think) in defense of their opinion, such as: "Christ is sitting at the right hand of the Father"; and "The flesh does not profit anything." These are indeed walls, but they are only strong enough to safeguard their opinion as snow is strong enough to provide heat. Despite the fact that they have published many pamphlets about this, they have been unable to create a good appearance on behalf of themselves for this one phrase of Paul: "… not discerning the Lord's body."

What, then, are we doing? We are not acting in secret nor are we teaching under a bushel. Listen briefly. This is what we are doing. We are coming together and eating the body of Christ in commemoration of the body of Christ, who died for us on the cross. In like manner, we are receiving the cup and are drinking the blood of Christ in commemoration of the blood of Christ which He shed for us in His suffering and death. We do and believe all these things according to the institution of Christ.

This is our naiveté in Christ, in which naiveté the serpent even today is leading away many people as it did Eve. We laugh and are misled to become absolutely insane people, namely, people who cannot know that bread is bread and one is one, something which common sense knows in sane people and as both Jews and Turks know. In addition, very many of the Sacramentarian books accuse us of being totally wicked as people who are teaching contrary to Scripture, contrary to the articles of faith, and of making and of creating for ourselves some made-of-bread-God, that is, as if we are saying that God was made bread, despite the fact that we are rather saying with Christ that the bread which we are eating in commemoration of Christ is the body of Christ. Therefore, Satan himself, however erudite he may be, still knows how to blaspheme with appropriate words so that not even by blaspheming something good and holy does he betray himself as the spirit of lying.

However, when they have made us wicked and have condemned our entire Gospel, they are also accusing themselves of having no love when we point out—even with a few words against those very many things which they are writing—that their errors and lies come from Satan. If (as far as they are concerned) the matter is against the consecrations of the papists who persecute the Gospel and yet boast of their anointings and tonsures, why are the Sacramentarians condemning the sincere professors and confessors of the Gospel?

But if someone requires a reason for this naiveté of ours, he should read Paul's first letter to the Corinthians (c. 11), where he speaks with clear words in favor of us. Also, we respond in this way, if perhaps our adversaries should even listen to us, for we want them (as well as others) to think of us as experienced people.

First, I said: "We come together," for Christ instituted this Sacrament in remembrance of Himself. As Paul explains it, it is the announcement of Christ's death. However, you will have announced this in vain when others are not present. We therefore come together, preach and chant, but with an understood chant[5] and one which even the common folk sing, and we pray as we acknowledge the death of Christ and give our thanks.

Furthermore, I said: "We receive the bread and eat the body of Christ, and we receive the cup and drink the blood of Christ; for Christ says: 'Do this.'" In this word, we do confidently what Christ has instituted. We do not trust in our consecrations and in our breath smelling of wine, as people foolishly object to us, but in the

---

5 That is, using a liturgy which is in the language of the people.

word of Christ: "Do this." That is, we trust in the institution and command of Christ.

Here, however, a disagreement has developed from these words. You see, the Sacramentarians explain "Do this" as follows: "Take the bread and eat the bread; take the wine and drink the wine." That's what those should say who don't want to see and hear what Christ says.

But we who are keeping the institution of Christ inviolate and are corrupting nothing of the words of institution speak in this way: "Christ took the bread and gave it to His disciples as He said: 'Take, eat; this is My body which is given for you. Do this. As often as you will have done this...'" That is: "Take the bread and eat My body, and believe that the bread which you are eating according to My institution in remembrance of Me is not simply bread but My body which is given for you." We also say: "In like manner, He took the cup and gave it to them as He said: 'All of you, drink of this; this is My blood, etc. Do this as often as you drink it in remembrance of Me.'" He says: "'Do this'; that is, take the cup, and drink My blood, and believe that the cup which you are drinking according to My institution in remembrance of Me is My blood."

Therefore Christ did not institute and say: "Do this"; that is: "Take and eat the bread. Take and drink the wine," but: "Do this." That is: "Take and eat My body. Thus I institute, thus I want, thus I command. Take and drink My blood. Thus I institute, thus I want, thus I command, so that in remembrance of Me you are drinking My blood. I am not instituting that in remembrance of Me you are eating simple bread, but that you believe that the bread which you are eating is My body. Similarly, I am not instituting that in remembrance of Me you are simply drinking the cup, but that you believe that the cup which you are drinking is My blood."

"Therefore, take and eat the bread which you are breaking among yourselves, which is My body. I am not saying nor ordering you to make My body with the bread but that you eat the bread, which is now My body. Take and drink the cup which you are distributing among yourselves, which is My blood. I am not saying nor ordering that you make this cup My blood, but that you drink the cup which is now My blood."

"I am instituting and want that in remembrance of My death you eat My body and drink My blood so that the bread which you eat often in remembrance of Me is My body and that the cup which you drink often in remembrance of Me is My blood."

"Therefore, come together for this sacred feast as often as you wish, act in remembrance of Me, preach Me, comfort yourselves mutually with a recollection of the blessings you have received through Me, give thanks regarding My death because I have given over My body on your behalf and I have shed My blood for you for the forgiveness of your sins."

This, briefly, is the institution of Christ, if you examine its action, Word, and command as is necessary. This is what He wants, what He institutes, and what He commands; namely, that, whenever it seems good, come together and eat His bread which He Himself says is His body, and drink His cup which He Himself says is His blood; then let us both eat and drink in remembrance of Him.

Here you have everything. We are not playing around with uncertain and inappropriate figures of speech as do the Sacramentarians, nor are we sacrificing a sacrifice and forbidding the laity from sharing what Christ instituted, as do the papists. Because we desire to be Christians, we add nothing to, nor do we take anything from, what Christ says, for we believe that this is true. We are doing what He Himself commands, and we are keeping inviolate and whole the institution of Christ just as we must.

The Christian has nothing to do with what reason and common sense contradict. That people say that these things are contrary to Scripture and the articles of faith can be said only by

Satan even if someone say them who is of the elect and is erring a second time. After all, Christians know that no Scripture and no article of faith is contrary to the word of Christ. On the contrary, Scripture commands under threat of the judgment of God that we hear this Prophet about whom the Father says: "Listen to Him." If you do not believe the words of Christ, you will have no Holy Scripture and no article of faith.

If now Christ is an offense to you in some one passage of His Gospel, He will become that in every passage. Those have given an egregious example of this who in their public writings boast with uncommon boasting that up to this point theologians have not understood correctly that passage of Paul in Rom. 5, which is about the sin which we call "original."

However, God shall have seen those things, and He shall defend the glory of His Son, who was handed over for us. Therefore, the Son Himself, who is in the glory of His Father, shall defend Himself. Moreover, let Him defend Himself through His customary mercy in order to confound the errors of men, and let Him save men. After all, far be it from us to call down the judgment of God upon anyone, for He is present with those who despise Him, and this of His own free will, while in the meantime, He is delivering with His gracious mercy those who err and sin.

Next, the commemoration of Christ (that is, the announcing of His death) does not require that external feast of Christ's body and blood, for it can and should take place often without this. After all, when should we not announce the Gospel? However, obviously we ought not celebrate this feast without the commemoration of Christ or the remembrance of His death, so that we do not embrace the Sacrament without faith (which I am in the habit of saying often). Christ did not say: "As often as you celebrate the remembrance of Me, etc.," but: "As often as you eat My bread and drink My cup, do this in remembrance of Me."

Those who embrace the Sacrament without faith are not so much the people who are ignorant of it nor who are unwilling to believe that the body and blood of Christ are there—for what concern would those have for the institution of Christ? Rather, those are the people who have been taught by the words of Christ and who believe that the body and blood of Christ are there and yet do not have faith in the death of Christ by which He Himself gave up His body and shed His blood for our sins, for this is what Scripture calls "Christian faith," namely, trusting in Christ.

The Corinthians believed that this bread of Christ was the body of Christ and that this cup of Christ was the blood of Christ. Paul says to them: "I speak to you as prudent people, that is, as people who understand the matter. You yourselves should judge what I am saying. The cup of blessing which we bless, is it not the communion of the blood of Christ? And the bread which we break, is it not the communion of the body of Christ?" [1 Cor. 10:15–16] And yet, there was that abuse in some that they despised the poor and perplexed with their feasts those who had no such wealth, that they became drunk to the great offense of others, that disagreements arose among those, and that they otherwise would eat the sacrifices to idols to the offense of the weak, etc. Paul rebuked those without faith (that is, without trust in Christ and in the blood of Christ) because they had abused the body and blood of Christ. You see, those who have faith in Christ cannot do those things to the contempt, confusion, and offense of others, nor can they stir up disagreements and sects nor embrace them, regardless of what frail sinners they still are over against others.

Therefore, to come to this Sacrament with faith is not only to believe that the body and blood of the Lord are here, something which the words of Christ have: "This is My body; this is My blood"; with which words He did not play around and did not lie. Moreover, this entire action, command, and word of His do not ad-

mit any figurative language. Rather, it also means that you have confidence in the death and blood of Christ, something which Christ
wanted when He said: "This do in remembrance of Me."

Christ did not want a cold or hypocritical commemoration
(that is, the announcement of His death) among His disciples, but
that what we announce with our mouth that we believe with our
heart that He was offered for our salvation. He wanted this confidence of ours in Himself when He instituted this Sacrament in
commemoration of Himself.

It is not enough that our faith be Christian if you believe
that it is true and not a lie that God became incarnate from a virgin,
that He died and rose again and is seated at the right hand of the
Father, and that the Father, Son, and Holy Spirit are one God, etc.;
unless you have confidence in all these and that you believe that
these are yours through the grace of God—because the devil also
believes them, but he cannot have this confidence.

Thus, it is not enough for the Christian faith to believe
that the bread of Christ is the body of Christ and that the cup of
Christ is the blood of Christ unless you use this body and blood of
His just as He himself instituted and commanded us to use it. He
did not only say: "The bread is My body, and the cup is My blood,"
so that the papists may make out of this Sacrament whatever they
please because it contains such divine things; but He also added:
"Do this in remembrance of Me. Do this, that is, take and eat the
bread, which is My body on the basis of My institution; take and
drink the cup, which is My blood on the basis of My institution,
and do this in commemoration of Me, that you may both have and
announce confidence in my death and blood."

Therefore it is necessary that Christians not only know
what this Sacrament is, but also why it exists and how they must
use it—all of which the institution of Christ has expressed. Here
Christian faith does not dally over the things which it hasn't ex-

pressed while others grow weak over useless and empty questions. Furthermore, it would have been wicked here to neglect what that institution has expressed just as it also would have been no less wicked to throw out or add to it what so clear an institution did not include in its own words. Furthermore, it is wicked to change, twist, or adapt the sacred words so that this is not what Christ instituted.

Therefore people commit two sins here, for some neglect what this is. This is the body and blood of Christ because of the institution and will of Christ. Others abuse it because they confess and believe this here because of the words of Christ, just as some of the Corinthians did.

Therefore Paul says: "A person should examine himself, and so eat and drink of the bread and cup," not in just any way but in that way, namely, in the way of the Lord about which the Lord Himself declared: "This is My body; this is My blood." I say: "A person should examine himself" as to what faith or confidence he may have in the blood of Christ, the commemoration of which he should be doing lest without this confidence he eat and drink unworthily the body and blood of Christ to judgment for himself. He believes that these are present because of the words of Christ, but in the meantime, he does not distinguish the body of Christ, that is, he does not discern it. He comes to it not at all aware that this is a matter of his salvation, but as if he were coming to any other food. God does not suffer this contempt in His people. Therefore, Paul adds: "For this reason many among you are weak and sick, and many sleep, etc." [1 Cor. 12:30]

As I have said, such were some Corinthians who were believing that it was the body and blood of Christ which they were eating and drinking according to the institution of Christ; and yet, they were fostering disagreements and sects, and to the offense of others, were becoming drunk in the holy congregation. Also, they were not only not dividing their feasts with the poor who were standing or sitting in the Church or congregation, but even were confusing them through those meals and shaming those who didn't have money to do the same. True faith (that is, confidence in Christ) cannot do these and similar things.

Moreover, when they had eaten the common supper (which supper in the beginning the Corinthians used to call "the Lord's supper" because they were doing that in imitation of the Lord's Last Supper, even admitting those who were poor whom they later would not admit because of their greed and contempt for the poor), those who had eaten the supper received the body and blood of the Lord in imitation of the Lord's Supper.

Here those who neglected their own salvation and were unmindful of their own faith were receiving the body and blood of the Lord with no greater attention than when they had received the preceding supper. This is "not discerning the Lord's body," just as many experts on the Mass among us have ultimately treated this Sacrament with contempt because of habit itself, although I, who am comparing these to those Corinthians, do not see why they have done that. For what else are these but experts on the Mass? They sinned in some way or another, but they wanted to commune according to the institution of Christ.

However, it is very beautiful that we hear that some quite learned people among the experts on the Mass say (when they have read the books of the Sacramentarians): "Granted, if the body of Christ were in the Sacrament, we would have to change the Masses, for we are forced to admit our abuse; nevertheless, why wouldn't the body of Christ remain there, and why wouldn't we celebrate the Mass as we did before if the body of Christ is not present there, as some people are now contending? What danger would there be for us then?"

Do you see then this terrible wickedness? Must we fear that some are not celebrating the Mass with that confidence? But who

46

will deliver those who before were anxious without faith but now are despisers from the sentence of Paul (which will always stand strongly against those and will not permit them to go without upset hearts and bad consciences), even if they should believe that the body and blood of the Lord are not there? He says: "He who has eaten this bread and drunk the cup of the Lord unworthily will be guilty of the body and blood of the Lord, and eat judgment for himself, not discerning the body of the Lord." [1 Cor. 12:29] Therefore, people without faith will always need their preparations and will struggle with their anxious consciences as before.

However, if they will have held the words of Paul in contempt, tell me please, with what confidence will they pretend before the laity that they are sacrificing the Son of God for the living and the dead if they have mocked so much the bread and wine before the eyes of others? They should be careful of their ambition and profits, for they have determined to despise God and people. You see, when the laity, who generally have better consciences in this area (for they are seeking neither gain nor high office from this) have discovered this, they will readily abstain from the Masses of their priests, regardless of who conducts them, and they will be compelled to suspect all the priests. You see, they will be compelled to suspect it is true of all their priests what is said about some of them, namely, that they are not handling the body and blood of the Lord but are mocking the bread and wine as men who are hating, blaspheming, and prosecuting whatever of the Sacraments that belong to us and who hate the righteousness of Christ or faith and the Gospel.

Up to this point, God has endured the ignorance of good consciences; but what ignorance is there, now that the Gospel has been revealed through Christ?

However, we are saying these things to those who embrace the sacred Gospel of Christ as the Corinthians did at that time when they did not eat the most sacred body of Christ and drink

His blood unworthily to their damnation, as some of the Corinthians were doing at that time who (in addition to the things of which we have spoken) were dealing with others in an insufficiently sacred way, as we may see in 1 Corinthians.

You have what our examination is that we may approach [the Sacrament] in a worthy way, something which the Lord wanted to commend to us when He commanded that we eat and drink in remembrance of Him; namely, that we not receive the Sacrament without faith.

"But," you say, "if we don't have confidence in your consecrations, flatulence, and fetid breath" (What blasphemies are we not compelled to hear?) "why, when you are about to chant the words of Christ: 'This is My body; this is My blood,' do you bring forth the bread and wine and in this way blaspheme God in the bread that you may create some 'bread-God?'"

I respond. I leave to the blasphemers their blasphemies that they may blaspheme still more, if in this way it seemed best to Christ our Lord that He suffer those, for He is the Judge of the living and the dead. I also am responding only to that question which is being asked for the sake of those brothers who perhaps had been desiring an answer. In the presence of those who are unwilling to hear anything other than what they conceived to create, it is wiser and therefore more godly to remain silent than to speak.

We are not only repeating over the bread and wine those words of Christ: "This is My body; this is My blood," but we are also repeating the entire institution or ordination of Christ in this way: "Our Lord Jesus Christ, on the night when He was betrayed, took bread, gave thanks, broke it and gave it to His disciples. He said: 'Take and eat. This is My body which is given for you. Do this in remembrance of Me.' In the same way, He took the cup after supper, gave thanks, and gave it to them saying: 'All of you, drink of this. This cup is the new testament in My blood, which is shed for

48

you for the remission of sins. Do this, as often as you drink it, in remembrance of Me."' [1 Cor. 12:23–25]

We repeat all these words over the bread and the cup that the prerogative of our Ruler—namely, the institution and ordination of our Lord Jesus Christ—may endure to the end of the world among the faithful; that is, as Paul says, "…until He come." [1 Cor. 12:26] When we come together, we do not desire to eat here common bread or to drink common wine, but that bread which Paul calls "the bread of the Lord," that is, of Christ, and that cup which Paul calls the cup of the Lord, that is, that bread and that cup which Christ instituted for us to eat and drink in remembrance of Him.

This bread and cup before [the consecration] were common bread and cup—things which anyone, both worthy and unworthy, even dogs and pigs, were permitted to eat without danger or, if you prefer, without discrimination, provided that people not be concerned over the disgrace of their Creator. But when that bread and cup have come to the institution of Christ so that we may come together and eat and drink in remembrance of Christ, then it is no longer common bread but rather it is the bread of the Lord, and no longer common cup, but the cup of the Lord, not in the same way that the earth and its fullness are the Lord's, but in a unique way so that each person who eats this bread and drinks this cup unworthily becomes guilty of the body and blood of the Lord, and eats damnation for himself.

Because the Sacramentarians deny these things, I ask them here in passing: on what basis, with what breath, with what words, with what magic spell (I am omitting other blasphemies) does their bread and cup become so sacred in the remembrance of Christ that the person who uses them unworthily brings judgment upon himself and becomes guilty of the body and blood of the Lord? If they may have said that which I do not doubt the more sane are going to say, namely, that this happens because of the institution of Christ;

then I thank them, providing they also cease responding to us in this case the way they have been.

That I may express here the holiness and usefulness of this bread and cup of our Lord Jesus Christ from the words of Paul, I am adding here (even against the will of our adversaries who are crying out that there is no usefulness of the flesh here) the following: If someone eats and drinks unworthily, he becomes guilty of the body and blood of the Lord. From this it follows that anyone who eats and drinks worthily becomes a partaker of the body and blood of the Lord. But now, who is ignorant of how great are the majesty and sanctity of the body and blood of the Lord, of which in the meantime the person who eats worthily this bread and drinks this cup becomes a partaker thereof? Paul says this very thing: "The bread which we break, is it not the communion of the body of the Lord? The cup of blessing which we bless, is it not the communion of the blood of Christ?" [1 Cor. 10:16] Also, if anyone eats and drinks unworthily, he eats and drinks damnation for himself, not discerning the Lord's body. From this, it follows that whoever eats and drinks worthily eats and drinks salvation for Himself, discerning and recognizing the Lord's body.

However, that you not be unaware of what "participation" or "communion of the body and blood of Christ" as well as of what "discernment" Paul is speaking (because I also see these being corrupted), ask the institution of Christ which says: "That bread is My body; that cup is My blood. The former is handed over or broken for you, and the latter is shed for you for the remission of your sins."

What is our source for all these points? They come from the institution of Christ. He Himself in this way instituted, ordained, and wanted them. Christians accept this institution and give thanks for it. Therefore, it would be foolish to omit these words of the institution of Christ, and wicked to not trust them, for without these words, what would we be looking for in the bread and cup?

The minister of our Church recites publicly these words of Christ's sacred institution over the bread and cup which have been placed upon the table or altar, without his breathing upon them (as people laugh about us), when he acknowledges that his own power is accomplishing nothing here, but that everything that happens is happening by the power of Christ's institution and ordination.

First, those who are about to commune (unless they be present, there is never a Mass for us), and also our Church, gathered as it is in Christ for the Gospel, prayer, and hymns, should acknowledge what we must do and believe with regard to this Sacrament. You see, Christians presume nothing here that Christ neither commands nor says, just as they cannot hold in contempt any of those things which He commands or says. What does He command? "Take, eat, and drink in remembrance of Me." What does He say or declare? "This is My body, etc.; this is My blood, etc." We must do the former; we must believe the latter. Both, however, are the work of God; for it is by His power that we believe the words of Christ. If He shall have given us grace, we shall do what He commands here; that is, we shall eat the bread and drink the cup of Christ worthily in remembrance of Him and certainly not in a hypocritical manner, as we said earlier.

Next, we do not conceal the words of the institution of Christ so that even the papists finally may learn that we must not abuse the Sacrament and that the experts in the Mass may come to their senses and return from their wicked Masses to the unity of holy mother Church which can take up nothing else for salvation than the Gospel of Christ. Nothing holds them away from the Gospel more than those Masses from which (for the sake of their ambition and profit or at least superstition) they have made a sacrifice and work of satisfaction for the living and the dead when they themselves eat and drink. They are permitting to others only what they see but not to eat and drink and, in fact, even judge them as heretics if any may have been willing to drink according to Christ's institution.

Those experts say that the laity should listen to the Mass and that the cup cannot even be received by the laity. You will hear anything you want in those Masses except those things which have truly been sent, that is, the institution of Christ, which they announce as a work done so that they are not even listening to themselves for this alone, namely, that others may not hear it.

Therefore, they must learn that this Sacrament can be nothing other than what Christ wanted and instituted it to be, and that is something we must see and understand from His words. For whatever else you may have made of it is wrong, fictitious, and wicked. It is nothing that you believe is here. Believe the institution of Christ which has nothing unclear if you have been seeking the truth. Oh, how far have people erred in their abuse of this Sacrament!

Now that we have revealed the error, you must continue to have a bad conscience, you expert in the Mass. There is no place for excuse. Your wickedness can spread out a pretense before people, but see constantly what your conscience may respond to you in the presence of God.

Furthermore, the Christian Church must hear these words of the institution of Christ publicly today so that the Sacramentarians not cry themselves hoarse against us as regards under what order and under what power "you are making the body of Christ." Therefore I am keeping their blasphemies silent here, for this institution responds endlessly against them and on our behalf. Also, the ordination of Christ is going to endure until the end of the world, for it causes us to eat and drink the body and blood of Christ. It neither demands nor commands that we 'make' the body and blood of Christ, which is *given* to us and which we *receive* with a grateful heart and with exultant thanksgiving. We are not presuming to do what we cannot do, for Christ does not command us to do that, for He says: "This is My body; this is My blood." He does not say: "Make My body; make My blood." He did not want *makers* of His body and blood, but wants *sharers* thereof, that is, that we eat the Lord's body and blood in remembrance of Him, because He *gives* this body and blood to us through His institution—not that we should *make* them for ourselves.

If it pleases you, repeat to me here the very works of God's creation and whatever God ever instituted or ordained from the beginning of the world. Tell me when He ever did anything without His arrangement, not to mention when He ever declared anything which was not true or which was not the eternal truth. He spoke, and they were done; He commanded, and they were created. O Lord, may Your Word remain in heaven forever, may Your truth endure from generation to generation! You laid the foundation for the earth, and it endures. Your judgments have endured until now, because all things serve You.

In this way, God created light with His Word. He arranged that the sun rise daily and it cannot help but set; for He divided it from darkness, and there cannot be a sharing of light with darkness forever. Why? Because God once instituted and ordained this with His Word. Therefore light can never lack His arrangement and institution, for the eternal truth cannot deny itself.

What God once created and instituted endures and acts and works in its own times in this way and has its effectiveness just as He originally commanded with His Word. It has persisted just as long as He Himself wished at that time when He instituted and ordained it. All things stand and fall according to His Word, just as He said. All the days of the earth, sowing and harvesting, cold and heat, summer and winter, night and day will not rest.

Who today creates men and living things? Who multiples the crops? Who therefore raises them up again when they have been lost and have died upon the earth? Who gives the trees their foliage and fruits? Who gives all these the power to produce of themselves things similar to themselves? Isn't it the arrangement [or institution] of God which commands all these to have within themselves their seed?

By whose Word and power all things were first created, by His Word and power today all things are born and controlled and persist just as He prescribed to them with His institution a long time ago. All things which have been created have their effectiveness from the creating and instituting Word of God so that you see that God and His Word have never been idle nor ineffective, and this in His own times and in His own way which He said once, as Christ says: "My Father works until now, and I am working." [John 5:17]

Therefore, when the faithful person directs his attention to matters, he wonders at all things. He wonders at the annual return of the sun, he wonders at the monthly departure of the moon, at the variety of the stars, at the changes of the times, at the various changes of living creatures, regions and all things. He wonders how water extinguishes thirst, how bread nourishes, how cows (but not people) eat hay and fodder, how people cannot live in water and fishes cannot live outside water, how birds are carried in the air. Briefly, the faithful person sees that pure miracles fill the whole world wherever he turns, and even that he himself and all his life are nothing else but wonderful works of God, as the psalmist sings, saying: "O Lord, You have delighted me with Your work, and I shall exult in the work of Your hands. How magnificent are Your works, O Lord, and Your thoughts are very deep. The senseless person will not recognize this, nor will the foolish one understand it." [Psa. 92:4–6]

In all these things, the faithful person acknowledges the eternal power, wisdom, goodness, and providence of the invisible God toward those things which He has created. Briefly, the believer acknowledges the infinite majesty and divinity of God (Rom. 1). Finally, when through these things, as with a ladder and its rungs, faith has entered into the sanctuary of God, he ceases to wonder and says: "It is not strange that He has set these wondrous things before our eyes, because the omnipotent and eternal Word of God through which all things were made and without which nothing was made has made all these things." In God they are not miracles, but all the things which He makes and preserves with His Word are miracles in our eyes, just as it is said about Christ, at first damned but soon glorified: "That was done by our Lord, and it is wondrous in our eyes."

You see here, don't you, how broad and open this field is for me for speaking about the creation and providence of God and about all things which God has ever said? He has done and is doing all things with His Word, whatever He has done and is doing. If I were free to write many words, I certainly would do this without empty figures of speech, that is, without the sort of tropes which are not posited in this text and without seeking them anxiously and twisting Scripture into a foreign meaning. In addition, I would not misquote the ancient writers with my lies—as I see that all these things are now happening quite unjustly in the Sacramentarian cause.

Satan is seeking that he himself receive worship not as the Word of God but under the guise of the Word of God, as you see his customary behavior (Mat. 4). I would act, however, with absolutely certain Scripture and with absolutely certain, palpable, or even visible arguments. Now it is enough to have indicated the truth and to have given an opportunity to a wise person, not only for the sake of brevity but also, as I admit naively, that I am not sufficiently suitable to describe these miracles of God; but then, who can be sufficiently suitable for this?

At this time, we only wanted to indicate that the faithful know that it is the omnipotent and eternal Word of God which is performing these miracles, that the eternal truth is God, and that His eternal power cannot be absent from His Word and institution. In fact, whatever He may do He does in His own time and in His own way, and that includes what He once created with His own Word and which He arranged to happen in His own time. Take away that efficacy of His Word from creatures, and they are instantly nothing.

However, if God is never without His arrangement and institution, if what He Himself said is ever true, if He always accomplished what He wanted with His Word, why do the Sacramentarians rail wickedly at just this one institution of Christ, tear it up into a thousand pieces and, briefly, deny that this is something which Christ instituted? This is not the place for those figures of speech. If you pay attention to this entire institution, if you snatch it this way and that way now through little bits of it and thus confuse its meaning, you are showing contempt for the will of Him who did the instituting.

Is not Christ God? Is not He Himself that eternal and omnipotent Word who created all things, and who continues and preserves all things? He says: "The bread which I am handing you, which I want you to eat in remembrance of Me, is My body; and I am instituting that, as often as you wish, you eat My body. The cup which I am handing you, which I want you to drink in remembrance of Me, is My blood which is shed for you for the remission of sins. I am instituting that, as often as you wish, you drink My blood by the authority of My command and institution." And you—are you wickedly blaspheming the source from which you will receive the body and blood of Christ?

[The Sacramentarians say:] "Who has given you the power to make the body of Christ (I am not mentioning the made-of-bread-God)? Do you think that at the foul breath of the mouth of anyone, or at the agreement and will of even a fornicator or adulterer or usurer, Christ is carried around hither and yon and is abandoning the throne of His majesty?" Say, you wicked and blasphemous person, yes, you who are deserting the word of Christ, what are you doing to yourself and to the name "Christian?" Because you are unwilling to see what He has instituted and are having respect only for those things which seem to your reason to be absurd and impossible, you are opposing your reason to the word of Christ in an egregious and unchristian way.

From this you argue in this way: "You cannot make the body of Christ. Must it then be that those are doing a good thing who make fornicators? Is then the bread of Christ not the body of Christ?" Today we are compelled to endure those very shameless flowery speeches of Satan. O, you blaspheming Satan and your blasphemies! Because we are not making the body of Christ, will what Christ says ("The bread is My body; the cup is My blood") not be true? Is it by no means possible that what Christ orders and institutes happens, namely, that we receive and eat and drink His body and blood? Thus, those who love to make their dreams public after abandoning the absolutely certain word of Christ bump and run against the stone of offense.

But now, if you will, take a look at all the precepts of God. Tell me, please, when was God never present at one command of His? From whence, then, does He see that it is His commandment?

I don't want you to throw it up to me that God indeed gives people commandments but that people do not obey, for they either hold the commandment in contempt or they are unable to obey it, as when the entire Decalogue demands a pure mouth, which happens when it is a stranger to every concupiscence and which seeks not its own desires but what God and others seek. The precept is indeed for such people but it is not a precept of God for us. That is, as despisers, they do not accept nor understand it; and as hypocrites, they do not love it. Although they may try, because they are without faith, they do not provide what the Law demands, "for an evil tree cannot produce good fruits" [Mat. 7:18].

I say that this is a command of God among those who, how-ever frail they may be and however much they still don't acknowledge that they are obedient, nevertheless love and accept it as a command of their Lord and, therefore, who don't despise their Father and fol-low only the hypocrisy of the Law as Pharisaic righteousness. About these, we read in the Psalm [112:1]:"Blessed is the person who fears the Lord and takes delight in His commandments." These are the faithful, the good trees, whose hearts God has changed through His Spirit that they desire and love the commandments of God. About these, Christ also says:"He who has and keeps My commandments is a person who also loves Me." [John 14:21]

Tell me, therefore, when is God ever not present to His commandment, that is, where He sees that it is truly His com-mandment? He commands things which are impossible for the flesh, and He is present to His faithful, doing through them what they themselves could not do through their own nature without the Spirit. He does not impute to His beloved children whatever they do not do or whatever they do insufficiently, so that the whole Law and all the commandments of God are fulfilled in them. In this way, they make satisfactions through grace to the Law and to the will of God who is commanding them. The result is that the Law cannot demand more from them. Therefore, the Law has been abrogated and is dead for them when they are obedient to the will of their Fa-ther without the command of the Law. In the meantime, however, all other people who do not have the Spirit of God are acting under the transgression and condemnation of the Law, whether they may appear to be acting well or badly. For, as Paul says, "Whatsoever is not of faith is sin." [Rom 14:23] You see, the fruit of a corrupt tree (that is, of an unbelieving person) is corrupt, even if you should swear that his life is angelic.

God wants a pure (that is, a faithful) heart, without which all things, even those which on their face are very good, are impure before God and pure hypocrisy. After all, who will offer a pure heart except that One to whom it is said: "Create in me a pure heart, O God and renew within me a right spirit?" (Psa. 51:20) Such a heart, purified as it is by faith, loves the Law or the commandments of God. Therefore, God is present there that believers do the things the Law demands; I say, they do them without a law, that is, without the demand of a law through which demand believers can never do those things which a law demands. You see, they cannot please God with forced service. This is the grace and freedom of Christians in the Spirit through Jesus Christ our Lord.

If, then, among His faithful to whom He had given by His grace faith and a heart which loves the Law or the commandments God is never lacking His command or order, even when He has commanded impossible things for an unbelieving person, for all things are possible not to the natural person but to the believer; I say, if all this is so, why does Christ appear to you to be lacking His command here which you see in this sacred institution?

Here He is not commanding all people as He does in the Decalogue, but only His disciples who accept or seem to accept the Gospel, that is, His Church on earth. They do not despise His command; otherwise they would not want to be or to be considered His disciples. He is not commanding impossible things but even things which are pleasing to the flesh, and all the more to the spirit, when we are sure from the Word of God that these things are God-pleasing. He commands: "Take," and we take. He commands: "Eat. Drink," and we eat and drink. What is easier, what is more pleasant, than to have an invitation from the Word of God to those things which those who hunger and thirst seek in addition and which they are sorry are being denied to them? Here the Lord wants justice for those who hunger and thirst and not for those who abound in the spirit in such a lying way that they despise the institution of Christ.

Furthermore, He commands that we do these things "in remembrance" of Him. Tell me, please, what is sweeter than to come to such a much-desired feast with such pleasant companions and guests, namely, the sort of people who acknowledge that they are your brothers and who desire to die one for another or admit that they ought to do this, however much they still cannot do this because of the frailty of their flesh? Who would not want such tablemates who feel nothing other than the very best for each another? In addition, what is more filled with consolation, what is more salutary against every temptation, against every distress and poverty or need, against all sins, against human traditions and the doctrines of demons, against false theologians and all spiritual wickedness, that can be heard among Christians than the remembrance of the Lord, that is, than the announcement of Christ? For "God, the Father of mercies, who did not spare His own Son but handed Him over for us all, how will He not with Him give us all things?" [Rom. 8:23] Who now will bring an accusation against the elect of God, etc.?

Therefore, when Christ has instituted so healthy and sweet a feast, when so many and such pleasant associates or guests are present, when such useful, holy, and salutary congregating occurs among us, namely, that remembrance than which Christians hold nothing more sacred, through which all things are holy for them, through which they acknowledge that they are the children of God and that God is their Father, when there is nothing difficult here but where all things are even to be hungered after; I say, when all this is present, what Christian would not want to do or would not do those things which Christ commands here? Only those who despise themselves either never come or, if they do come, do not do what Christ has commanded, even if they eat and drink the Lord's Sacrament.

However, if we come together for this sacred institution of Christ so that we disciples of the Gospel may do what our Master

Christ has commanded; tell me, please, whether Christ here can do without His institution and the desire of His obedient disciples? We believe that His institution is good, holy, true, and salutary for us; for in it Christ declares, promises, and gives us the remission of our sins, to wit, that ransom offered on the cross for us to God the Father in the fragrance of sweetness. Therefore, we come together for this institution and we are obedient to the will of Him who instituted it, for He commanded us and said: "This do in remembrance of Me. This do, that is, take and eat, this is My body; take and drink, this is My blood."

There we wish to eat the body of the Lord and to drink His blood not by some human invention nor by our own rashness and presumption, but by the institution and command of Christ, our Lord and only Master, who said: "This bread is My body. Take and eat My body which is broken for you. This cup is My blood, which is shed for you for the remission of your sins. Take and drink My blood, etc. For I want you to do this, provided you do it in remembrance of Me, until the end of the world, that is, until I come, but in the meantime, as often as you may have wished."

Christ is attentive to this gathering of ours, to this will and desire of ours as the Institutor and Grantor of this gift. He is also present through His Word, from which it cannot be absent in this institution. It is He who gives us His body and His blood, for "The bread is My body" and "The cup is My blood" are not our words but His who created all things with His omnipotent Word and who with His Word has done everything He wanted to do.

Although this happens visibly through the hand of His minister, nevertheless we receive invisibly from the hand of Christ by the power and efficacy of His institution or His Word the body and blood of Christ. Hasn't He Himself promised: "Where two or three are gathered together in My name, there I am in the midst of them"? [Mat. 18:20] And don't we gather together in the name of

Christ when we come together to His institution, believing what
He said and doing what He Himself commanded? Therefore He
is there and gives us His body and blood and in this way preserves
His institution and the truthfulness of His word.

His institution cannot deceive. His Word cannot be a
lie, and the disciples who follow His Word cannot be wrong lest
you ask endlessly: "From what source will you receive the body of
Christ? Perhaps you are looking at the hands of some fornicator to
make the body of Christ for you, etc."

I omit the rest of the blasphemies which indicate sufficiently what little faith you have, and yet you require in us modesty
when we detect errors and accuse the lying spirits and propose clear
Scripture or the frank words of Christ. May God cause us to be truly modest so that our modesty becomes well-known to all people,
but may He forbid the mercy of Christ in us that we not deceive
others with our feigned modesty and turn away from the truthfulness of the Word of God. We are now seeing in some people the
sort of modesty which boasts that it is true modesty. To an intel-
ligent person the actual boasting indicates sufficiently what it is.

Up to this point, we have been sufficiently deceived by a
humility which is well-adapted to deceit and by an angelic religion
of those who were puffed up in their spirit in those things which
they were not seeing; that is, they were only dreaming it or even
imagining it to themselves, for they were not understanding nor believing or certainly were doubting. Paul is teaching us to be careful
of these (Col. 2 [:18 ff.]), so that there is no need for us to take up
the same again under another disguise, swollen up in vain as they
are over those things which they have not seen, that is, about matters of which they themselves are terribly uncertain.

Therefore, that you not pretend something impossible in
this sacred command of Christ which says: "Eat My body; drink
My blood"; and that you not say that it was very easy to take the

bread and the cup and eat and drink; that Christian gathering together and salutary remembrance of Christ are pleasant, and we
must seek all these things, especially Christ, who has in this way
instituted them. But who will make or pretend that bread to be the
body of Christ and the cup to be His blood that I may respond to
the command of Christ by which He orders me to eat here His
body and drink His blood? It seems impossible to me to command
that I eat and drink here things which cannot be here, things which
no one can make. If I were to attribute anything to the merit of His
ministers (something which the Christian faith does not know),
nonetheless who will apprise me of the merit of the minister that
I may know when the body of Christ is present there? I say, do not
pretend this and do not say these things. Christ is the true Wisdom
of God. He knows what, for whom, and how He has instituted and
commanded something, and He reveals Himself through His own
body and blood when He says: "The bread is My body; the cup is
My blood. I am not commanding you to make My body and blood
but that you eat My body and drink My blood."

That you not pretend such a horror when you have the
command to eat His human body and drink His human blood,
He makes the bread His body and the cup His blood in this sacred institution in such a way that your senses are not horrified any
more than you shudder at bread and wine when you are hungry
and thirsty. That's how easy it is to eat the body of Christ and drink
His blood, provided that in the meantime you do not come to them
with listless contempt, but discern the body and blood of the Lord.
You see, the same bread which you are eating here is His body and
the same cup which you are drinking here is His blood because of
His institution.

Therefore, when Christ institutes and commands that we
eat and drink here His body and blood in remembrance of Him,
what Christian would lead us to a neglect of this? When He com-

mands such easy, such pleasant, such salutary things and such things that we should also seek them out, what clearly wicked person could despise this or pretend a difficulty or even an impossibility, especially when He is commanding only that we do this as often as we may have wished?

However, when we disciples of Christ are not neglectful and do not hold it in contempt, but come together for the sacred institution of Christ, intending to do and receive what Christ institutes, do you think that Christ is not present with His disciples, that is, with His Church which has gathered together in this way that she does not desire to have any teacher except her Schoolmaster, who is Christ? Do you think that there is no concern there that what He Himself institutes become true? Do you think that He is going to permit His institution to be a lie and deceive as many as have received it? Quite obviously we have been wicked people and not the disciples of Christ, if we had suspected such things about that very sacred institution of His.

If some people may have said that they are weak and are unable as yet to grasp such things, they should not in the meantime become the schoolmasters of the world and upset good consciences which they cannot strengthen in their own opinion with the sure Word of God. We shall willingly consider them not as wicked but as weak brothers, provided they do not fall in love with their own ignorance, which is contempt for the Word of God.

If, however, God has never been lacking in regard to His institution and if He has always been present to those who are obedient to Him, obviously He is not going to be absent from this arrangement and command of His so that that which He Himself wanted, ordained, and instituted is impossible to come to pass with the result that the eternal truth through which He created all things becomes guilty of a lie. In what way, then, did that eternal truth institute and ordain those things?

To this add (should you wish) all the miracles of God which He ever commanded to take place through human beings. The saints have been obedient to God when He commands anything. According to the command of God, they have done some things in the manner of humans which human beings are unable to do. Therefore, God has been present, doing those things which the very saints, as human beings, had been unable to do.

In this way, Christ our Lord (who did all things by the command of His Father) intending to heal the man who had been blind from his birth, spat upon the ground, made mud out of His saliva, and smeared the mud upon the eyes of the blind man. He was able to do all these things as a human being, while nevertheless acknowledging that, as God, He wanted those things. How those would have laughed here who have nothing in their mouth about the very sacred Sacraments of Christ but contempt and blasphemy!

They would they have said: "What do those things have to do with the subject? What advantage do these words offer? That is, what power have they for opening one's eyes? Cannot Christ open their eyes without these very foolish and clearly ridiculous words, not to say without these completely unnecessary things?"

But when they make only a mockery out of that smearing, why did the blind man have to mutter something at the pool of Siloam where he bathed? Obviously, that water where he washed off that mud took away his blindness at the same time and gave light to the blind man, didn't it? Could the Elbe, the Rhine, and the Oder do that? Could the whole sea? If the touch of Christ does not heal him, how will Christ heal someone who has been lost? Therefore it is necessary that those who just glance at those matters and who have abandoned the Word of God with which these things agree say that God wants to work through such things, that He knows how to help the blind man and thus how to help others to whom this report is going to come, not to mention in the meantime that it pleases Him to make our wisdom foolish. Let us learn in this way to follow His will and not that which seems to us to be right. "He hides Himself from the wise and reveals Himself to the little children," [Mat. 11:25] that is, to fools who, because of His Word, make much of these things which the foolish cannot judge as foolish and which the world wishes to debate rather than to believe.

But getting back to the point, I say that Christ, as a man, could do for the blind man all these things which another human could not have done. In addition, however, as God and the omnipotent Word of God, He gave him sight. So much for this.

"He took bread, gave thanks, broke it, and gave it to His disciples…" Up to this point, I see only human activities. Then, as their Master, He commands: "Take, eat. This do in remembrance of Me." However, as God and as the eternal Word of God, He says: "This is My body which I am instituting, and I command you to eat it. Here or this is My blood, which I institute and command you to drink in remembrance of Me." Had He not said these words, there would be nothing over which we might disagree with the Sacramentarians, whose fiction will not stand without having had those words taken out of the context of the institution of Christ.

Some people, the report has it, have taught recently in another place very poorly that at that Last Supper the bread was indeed the body of Christ, but not now. Clearly man is remarkably stupid in this matter, although full of words, for he does not even see that the whole cause of all the Sacramentarians crashed which he thought he was defending. Those therefore have decided instead to write some sort of fiction to persuade others when they cannot persuade themselves, in order that their opinion which they had undertaken to defend not drive them to retreat.

But why am I saying these things about Christ? Why are we not looking rather at the blind man? This, after all, will come closer to what we are saying. That blind man with saliva smeared over his eyelids has this word of Christ that He will give him eyes and sight: "Go, wash in the pool of Siloam." But why? "Namely, that you may see." He didn't have to understand anything else. Christ did not say to him: "Go, make eyes for yourself"; or: "Give that water this power that when it washes you there, it may give you sight." Therefore, the blind man left and did what Christ had commanded him, and he returned, having sight. He could have left; he could have washed. Believing, he did the things which he was able to according to the word of Christ, and Christ was present with His Word, and with His divine power He gave him sight, for He cannot be absent from His Word.

Thus we have here the word of Christ; namely, His institution and command: "Do this"; that is, "Eat the bread which is My body; drink the cup which is My blood in remembrance of Me." He does not say: "*Make* My body," but: "This *is* My body, which I am commanding you to eat." As His obedient people, therefore, we can come together, we can take and eat and drink. Furthermore, that we may eat and drink His body and blood, He Himself, who cannot make or permit His institution to be a lie, as certainly as He would cure him so certainly did He heal him so that this blind man who was obedient to His Word had sight.

Ananias was sent to Paul to lay his hand on Paul by which to receive his sight. Another person could have put his hand upon him. However, God was present with His Word and restored sight for Paul. Here, what did the laying on of hands have to do with restoring sight? What happened elsewhere for the curing of the sick? In fact, what happened elsewhere for the giving of the Holy Spirit? Christ, who had ordered it to be done in this way, wanted that. That, therefore, could not help but have happened which He had said was going to happen through such actions.

He is present with His Word and also does through people the things which people cannot do by themselves, however distinguished they may be for their sanctity. In this case alone, we decide whether people who are taking up the mandate of Christ can perform it and whether His Word is true for believers as regards what it commands them to do, namely, to eat His body and drink His blood in this sacred Eucharist, as we call it.

Is it not Christian to do what Christ commands? If a human being neglects often what He is commanded, is it not Christian to believe that what Christ says is true? We eat the bread of the Lord and drink the cup of the Lord and we remember Christ our Lord, as we declare that His body was handed over into death for us and that His blood was shed for us for the remission of our sins. These things we do because He is presenting His body and cup and says: "Take, eat, drink in remembrance of Me." We believe that the bread which we are eating in this way by order and institution of Christ and the cup which we are drinking in this way are the body and blood of our Lord Jesus Christ, because He Himself offers us His bread and says: "This is My body which is broken for you," and He himself offers us His cup and says: "This is My blood, etc." We are not believing in vain nor out of a superstitious dream of the human mind, but on the basis of Christ's Word. Heaven and earth will pass away, but not the words of Christ!

Why, then, are people suffering accusations either about an impossibility or about their sins where Christ is necessarily present and offering the truth of His word or institution?

If you will, take also something else from ancient history. The Lord tells Moses, Exo. 17[:5ff.]: "Go ahead of your people and take with you some of the elders of Israel. Take the rod with which you struck the sea into your hand and go. Behold, I shall stand there before you upon the rock in Horeb. You will strike the rock, and water will come forth from it that your people may drink." The account also adds the following: "And Moses did so before the elders of Israel." See also Num. 20[:7–10]: "The Lord spoke to Moses and said: 'Take your rod, gather your people and your brother, Aaron, and speak to the rock in their presence, and it will give water. And when you will have drawn water from the rock, the whole multitude and its beasts will drink.' Moses therefore took his rod which was in the sight of the Lord as He had commanded him, gathered the multitude before the rock, etc."

Moses here is listening to impossible, absurd, and laugh-provoking words (at which the wicked and unbelieving people undoubtedly laughed in secret), although, in the meantime, he is in very present danger of having the people stone him. Wouldn't Moses have despaired here, had God abandoned His Word by which He had promised water from the rock and looked solely at the realities of the situation? He surely might have said: "Water from a rock? We have nothing to drink! Who is this God who commands us to drink stones? That's some outstanding providence! Here finally is the hardness of the sand being turned into the nature of flowing water? Shall I accomplish this by striking the rock with my rod or staff? These instructions are like a game which fools and children play. Everyone will laugh at me, and they will stone me before these things happen."

However, Moses cast those absurd impossibilities from his eyes and looked upon the Word of God alone because God had commanded and said such things. Therefore, he did what God had commanded him. He gathered up his people, went ahead of them and led them to the rock. Because he had taken his rod with him, he spoke to the rock and struck it with his rod, because God had commanded him to do that: "Gather your people at the rock, take your rod, in front of your people speak to the rock and strike it with your rod." Moses was able to do these things according to the command of God that the rock might also pour forth water. No human could do this, but only the Word of God which had said: "The rock will give water." That word did not say: "Make water, Moses." Moses believed this Word and did what it had commanded him. But God was present with His Word and provided what He had said, just as He said: "I shall stand there before you above the rock in Horeb."

Thus we, too, do according to Christ's institution the things which He commands, and these certainly are very easy, pleasant things which Christians must seek after. We believe the things which He Himself speaks, for we have no doubt but that He is present with His institution and will provide the truthfulness of His Word no less certainly than He produced water from the rock at that time.

You see again how broad a field lies open before me here, were I to take pleasure in filling many pages with my words. Here it will have been enough to have indicated these points.

However, already for a long time, they [the Sacramentarians] have been chirping at me that all the miracles of God must be obvious so that our senses perceive them—otherwise they would not be miracles—but we see no such miracles in the Sacrament [of the Eucharist]. To these people, I respond: I have not produced these words about miracles to confirm whatever some people have made up regarding this Sacrament or whatever happens often as a result of the games of Satan, but to show that God could never have been absent from His Word.

The only miracle that we are proclaiming here is that the bread of the Lord is His body and that the cup of the Lord is His blood because of Christ's institution and word: "Eat, this is My body; drink, this is My blood." The word of Christ creates this miracle for us, but we are seeking no other miracle to see outside of this. Content as we are solely with the word of Christ, we occupy ourselves with no other miracles here. Here Christians respect only the word of Christ so that they believe what He says and declares, and do what He commands that they may be the true and obedient pupils of the one Schoolmaster. However, they do not see these things which are included in this sacred institution of Christ, and they think that nothing of them pertains to themselves, for what is it to Christians that people corrupt or make up stories about anything, except that Christians must refute errors with the Word of God?

Here in passing I should wish to admonish those who before wanted to appear to be our brothers that, when they are unable to restrain themselves, but rather write against the institution of Christ, they separate us from those who hate and persecute the Gospel in whose number they themselves admit we do not belong; second, that they write separately against us and not mix up everything in such a way that they pour upon our heads all the abuses and errors of all people for this one reason, namely, that we are unwilling to deny the institution of Christ in the last supper. For this reason, they have simply said that others are papists but that we are papists in two ways. I ask: What spirit endlessly snatches them up to condemn our entire Gospel, inasmuch as in the meantime we depart not even by a single word, as far as doctrine is concerned, from the truth of God, prepared as we are to receive an admonition even from a child if anything human touches us?

They should learn from those things which they object to in us about miracles which they do not perceive in a Christian way. They say that there is no miracle in the bread and cup of Christ because they see no miracle. Thus, they know that nothing separates the miracles and signs which are given to unbelievers from those which are given to believers.

Are those things not miracles to believers "which eye has not seen nor heard, which God has prepared for those who love Him [1 Cor. 2:9]?" These certainly are miracles about which they can never wonder enough: That the Gospel which had been hidden with God the Father from eternity has been revealed to them; that they receive the remission of sins through faith in Christ; that they acknowledge that they are the children of God; that they rejoice in tribulation; that they grow continually in faith and in the knowledge of our Lord Jesus Christ; that they know that in the resurrection their humble and cheap bodies will be reshaped in the brightness of the body of Christ, etc. These certainly are the sort of things which Peter says even the angels desired greatly to look into [1.1:12], and in proportion to which Paul says all human righteousnesses are "dung" [Phi. 3:8]. In fact, he is so amazed that he forgets the past and endlessly follows that he may ultimately be able to comprehend perfectly his knowledge of Christ, even as he is known. [Phi. 3:10–12]

Briefly, we are not demanding that you believe miracles here but that you believe the institution and word of Christ. If you are a Christian, you will not refuse a condition. If Christ is in the habit of being present at His creation, institution, and command that those things occur which otherwise could not occur, what rashness is it to want to exclude only *this* institution of Christ? What wickedness is it to make Christ a liar here? It is the height of foolishness to argue in this way: "You are incapable of making the body of Christ, because Christ did not say to you: 'Make My body.' What Christ says, therefore, is not true: 'The bread is My body; the cup is My blood,' unless one subvert the context of Christ's institution with false figures of speech."

You wish to hear that Christ, the Author of the Sacraments, is also their Giver, regardless of what sort the external minister thereof may be in secret. I should not pass judgment on the latter, for the Church of Christ does not suffer calumniators. If, however, she can correct them, she nevertheless does not commune with them. However, in the papist church, they are permitted to have such priests and to defend them. I therefore am speaking about the secret sinner who appears to be a good person and perhaps is a sort of Judas so that he preaches to me here the Gospel, not his own, but that of Christ, so that I believe not in the minister but in Christ so that he gives me not his own Sacraments but those of Christ. You see, had Christ not instituted such salutary Sacraments with His word, no ministers—neither good ones nor evil ones—could give me anything here nor be profitable to me.

In addition, listen to what I have been saying. Just as Christ baptizes us, so also He makes us one in this Sacrament with His body and blood (not to speak in common fashion).

That Baptism alone which John administered was called "the Baptism of John." Nevertheless, it was not a human invention but the plan of God, as we read in Luke 7[:29]. The Pharisees and experts in the Law rejected within themselves the plan [or counsel] of God and did not receive the Baptism of John. Christ says, Mat. 21[:25]: "Did the Baptism of John come from heaven or from men?" That is, was it the plan of God or an invention of men? We read in Luke 3[:2–3]: "The Word of the Lord came upon John in the wilderness, and he came into all the region of the Jordan, preaching the Baptism of repentance for the remission of sins." As a result, John himself says, John 1[:33]: "The One who sent me to baptize with water said to me, etc." In this way, he signified clearly that God had called him to preach and baptize. Furthermore, they were receiving Baptism from John that they might believe in Christ, who was going to come after him, as Paul says, Acts 19[:4]. Also, as John himself says, John 1[:31]: "He was revealed in Israel; for that reason I have come baptizing with water, etc."; and in Mat. 3[:11]: "I indeed baptize you with water unto repentance, etc."

But now (that you not throw up to us fornicators, homosexuals, and usurers, etc.) Baptism is of neither man nor angel but of Christ alone, regardless of the minister who administers it. As John the Baptist says [Mat. 3:11]: "He will baptize you with the Holy Spirit." If Christ baptizes, what judgment will you make within yourself regarding the man who administers it? Have respect for the hand of Christ! That you not say that these words were spoken about the Holy Spirit and not about water, Christ connected water to His Baptism as a necessary element (because He wanted to do that); and He said: "Except a person be born again of water and the Holy Spirit, etc." [John 3:3] With these words, He attributes regeneration not to the Spirit alone, but also to the water because of the Spirit, because with His Word or institution He wanted holy water for the faithful in their Baptism so that you do not cry out: "The flesh is not profitable for anything, and you are betraying your ignorance." If we are reborn with water, who does not see that Christ also baptizes us with water itself? The minister can indeed apply water to us, but no one can cause us to be born again of water save Christ alone with His Spirit.

Therefore you see that Christ Himself baptizes us with His Holy Spirit, even when a man is the minister of Baptism, not in his own name, but in the name of Christ. For this reason, you often read in Acts that the apostles and others baptized people in the name of our Lord Jesus Christ, something which Paul interprets in 1 Cor. [1:13] in this way, saying: "Let no one say that you were baptized in the name of Paul"; and in Gal. 3[:27]: "As many of you as have received Baptism have put on Christ," not the person who baptized you, not Mr. Jones or someone else, etc. And Rom. 6[:4]: "You were baptized into Christ Jesus and into the death of Christ Jesus." Peter also says, 1 Peter 3[:21]: "The Baptism of water saves us through the resurrection of Christ, etc."

Do you see that the apostles understood that Christ baptizes us through water? Paul speaks in this way, Eph. 5[:25–26]: "…Christ loved the Church and gave Himself for her to sanctify and cleanse her through the washing of water in the Word, etc." Doesn't he say also that Christ is in the water and, in fact, He baptizes with water, and that He baptizes with water in such a way that through the water He cleanses His bride? As we said before, the minister can indeed apply water, but he cannot regenerate or, as we read here, cleanse through the water. Moreover, what Christ said there: "…of water and the Holy Spirit," Paul says here: "…by the washing of water in the Word."

I am pointing to this because of some people who, when they read this now: "It is the Spirit who gives life"; and: "The words which I have spoken are Spirit and life," dream to themselves that those deceptive thoughts and fictions of the human heart are the Holy Spirit, and in this way boast of the fullness and overflowing of the Spirit. Thus we may see that they do not understand the words of God which express faith to us.

So, also, Paul says, Tit. 3[:5–6]: "…not by works of righteousness which we have done but according to His mercy He has saved us through the washing of regeneration and the renewal of the Holy Spirit, whom He poured upon us abundantly through Jesus Christ, our Savior." What does "the regeneration and renewal of the Holy Spirit" say but that it is clear from the aforementioned passages that those who have been prepared to either deny or corrupt what Christ instituted have nothing against which to bring false charges?

However, what is the good of dealing with such obvious subjects at such length? I say that they are obvious to those who are concerned with the Word of God and the reading of the writings of the apostles. On the contrary, in fact, don't we respect the institution of Christ by which He instituted and commanded Baptism, saying: "All power is given to Me in heaven and on earth. Go, therefore, and teach all nations, baptizing them in the name of the Father and of the Son and of the Holy Spirit"? [Mat. 28:18–19] You hear that He commands them to baptize as the ministers, not as the creators, of Baptism. He Himself therefore gives *His* Baptism, not the Baptism of the apostles, although He does this through the apostles. It is undoubtedly His Baptism who instituted Baptism with His eternal and omnipotent Word. For this reason we call it "the Baptism of Christ," as we indicated earlier.

You see, when you do act not in your name but in the name of another (as in the name of judges, rulers, etc.), then you are not acting but that person is in whose name you are acting, provided he has entrusted that to you and had the power the commit it to you so that you acted in his name. In this way, the legates of rulers act in the name of their rulers and are recognized as doing that. Thus Paul says about his Gospel: "We are performing an ambassadorship for God and are exhorting you as if God be exhorting you through us." [2 Cor. 5:20] As a result, we have those words: "Blessed by the King of Israel who comes in the name of the Lord." [John 12:13]

Moreover, the wicked teachers who do not have the Gospel but human traditions and the doctrines of demons are not coming in the name of God the Father but in their own name. They either are lying that they are the ambassadors of God or, if they have been called to the office of the Gospel, they proclaim and demand those things which the Lord did not command them. How much more bearable was that very wicked betrayer Judas, who, as he sought after his own advantages, nevertheless kept preaching the Gospel and did not snatch up his hearers into a headlong fall into damnation! However, the world should receive those who are the true ministers of God and whom it knows only how to despise, blaspheme, and condemn. In this way, those who don't want to receive a love of the truth receive lies when the Gospel was preached, just as Christ says: "I came in the name of My Father, and you did not receive Me. If another will have come in His name, you will receive him." [John 5:43] Christ said this to very fine, very wise, and very righteous Jews, as they appeared on the surface, but whom the faithlessness of their heart (that is, their cupidity or quest for profits and arrogance) was turning away from the Gospel of Christ.

If, then, we indeed baptize, but not in our own name, why do you respect the human being who baptized or the minister of water and not rather Him in whose name we baptize on the basis of the institution and command of Christ?

We baptize in the name of the Father and of the Son and of the Holy Spirit, that is, in the name of the holy Trinity just as the whole Trinity was revealed in the Baptism of Christ. It is not that we receive Baptism because Christ was baptized, but because Christ instituted that we be baptized. Is not the person who is baptized in the name of the Father and of the Son and of the Holy Spirit baptized in the name of God? Is not he who is baptized in the name of God the Father baptized in the name of God? Is not he who is baptized in the name of the Son baptized in the name of God? Furthermore, is not he who is baptized in the name of the Son baptized in the name of our Lord Jesus Christ, who is the Son of God the Father and who is God? Thus it is written often in Acts that people were baptized "in the name of our Lord Jesus Christ."

We do not read with what words the apostles baptized but in whose name they baptized. Christ had not prescribed to them the words except the preaching of the Gospel, but He did command them to baptize in the name of God, so that some do not need to excuse the apostles for baptizing in the name of our Lord Jesus Christ.

Next, He who is baptized in the name of the Holy Spirit is baptized in the name of God because the Holy Spirit is also the God in whom we believe, just as we believe in the Father and the Son. Again, he who is baptized in the name of God is baptized in the name of the Holy Trinity—Father, Son and Holy Spirit—because this Trinity, blessed forever, is no one else than God. He who is baptized in the name of the Father who is God, is baptized in the name of the holy Trinity, for we cannot understand God the Father without God the Son, from whom the Holy Spirit cannot be absent, for He is the Spirit of both.

So, too, he who is baptized in the name of the Son who is God, is baptized in the name of the holy Trinity, for we cannot understand God the Son without God the Father, from whom the Spirit of both cannot be absent. So, too, he who is baptized in the name of the Holy Spirit who is God and the third Person in the Trinity, is baptized in the name of the holy Trinity. The Holy Spirit is the Spirit of the Father and the Spirit of the Son, and this Triune God cannot be separated.

However, because the institutor and author of this Baptism is Christ, the apostles were baptizing in the name of our Lord Jesus Christ, and were signifying that Christ Himself was baptizing and regenerating even through the water and cleansing His bride with the washing of water in the Word; and that the apostles were His ministers for the preaching of the Gospel (not their own but His Gospel), and for the giving of Baptism (not their own but His Baptism).

After the apostles, however, because of the heretics who were denying the Trinity (as some kept denying that the Son is God while others were denying that the Spirit is God, and still others that neither is God), the Church of Christ and His spotless bride, that is, which accepted nothing else as necessary for salvation save the Word of God or the Holy Gospel, began to baptize with these prescribed words: "I baptize you in the name of the Father and of the Son and of the Holy Spirit." This she did that the people who were receiving Baptism might be certain that they had received a correct Baptism according to the institution of Christ and in no other name than the holy Trinity, which the heretics kept denying.

This custom of prescribed words endures in the Church even now. We should not change it rashly because with these words the minister is saying that he is doing nothing else than what Christ instituted and commanded him to do, as if the minister is saying: "Christ commanded: 'Baptize in the name of the Father and of the Son and of the Holy Spirit.' Behold, I am baptizing you not in my name, but in the name of the Father and of the Son and of the Holy

Spirit. It is God who is baptizing you. Our Lord Jesus Christ, who instituted that you be baptized in this way, is baptizing you. Receive Baptism in His name that you may be a Christian, baptized as you are into Christ. Regardless of what sort of a person I may be, in the meantime I am His minister."

As a result, everyone says that the child who receives Baptism becomes a Christian who before Baptism they confess was a heathen. Clearly, they perceive that the child is being baptized into Christ, not into the human who is administering the Baptism, and that the child is being baptized not by a human but by Christ.

To this is pertinent that before the Baptism of infants, on the basis of a sacred and therefore necessary custom, the Gospel is read: "Permit the little children to come to Me, and do not forbid them, for the kingdom of heaven is made of such." [Mat. 19:14] In this way we signify that we are offering our little children to Christ, because He Himself says: "Permit the little children to come to Me." But because He adds: "The kingdom of heaven is made of such," we are also offering them to Christ to receive Baptism. After all, if theirs is the kingdom of heaven, why would we deny them Baptism? Is it unworthy for one to receive Baptism to whom the kingdom of heaven belongs?

Therefore, whether children or adults are receiving Baptism, they are being baptized in the name of our Lord Jesus Christ, who is the Author and Institutor of Baptism. Also, they are baptized in the name of God or of the holy Trinity, just as Christ instituted.

Here the minister has great glory, for he stands and acts in Baptism in the stead of Christ and of the entire Trinity. The baptized person, however, has even greater glory because he is receiving Baptism from Christ our Lord and from the entire Trinity, and because there God is entering a covenant of eternal salvation with a human who was born a child of wrath, and this through the resurrection of our Lord Jesus Christ, as Peter says [1.3:21], provided the person remain in that covenant.

What fornicators, blasphemers, usurers, and scoundrels will you throw up to me here? We do not accept criminal-minded ministers, as does the papist church. Moreover, if there is some hidden Judas who in the meantime appears to be one of us, there is nothing to keep me from receiving the Gospel from a man who is a preacher, for the Gospel is not of a man but of our Lord Jesus Christ. Thus, when I receive Baptism from a man who is a minister of the Church, I am receiving the Baptism not of a man but of our Lord Jesus Christ.

Why am I making these points about Baptism? Obviously that it become clear that Christ baptizes us when we receive Baptism according to His institution and command. This is something we have made clear from the writings of the apostles and from Christ's institution.

It is a shame that Christians pay no attention to this glory of Baptism. In fact, those who are opposed to the Gospel or at least in this area of it (something which they cannot deny) rather forbid today that we baptize in the German language in the presence of Germans, namely, that those who are present understand what is being said. As the Church from the time of the apostles preached in all languages, so also she has baptized in Hebrew among Hebrew speakers, in Greek among the Greeks, in Persian among Persians, in Latin among Latin-speakers. We alone are not permitted to hear our own language in the Holy Baptism of Christ. It is as foolish to question in Latin those German people who don't know Latin, so that they may respond in their language to questions they don't understand, as it is foolish to preach the Gospel to them in Latin.

Moreover, just as Christ baptizes us—albeit through a minister—so also (as we have said), He gives us His body and blood in this very Holy Supper about which we are speaking, although through a minister. Let us see again the words of this institution, for they should satisfy the disciple of Christ about this matter, as we said earlier. Christ says: "Take and eat. This is My body. Take and drink, this is My blood." For what minister will you have regard, namely, whether he is good or evil or a fornicator or adulterer? To what mumbling or foul-smelling breath will you pay attention here? I am not mentioning the rest of the blasphemies for the sake of our Lord Jesus Christ, who here gives us His body and blood. Is this the word of the human minister: "Take and eat. This is My body," so that you are afraid you are about to receive the body of a fornicator or betrayer? Therefore, we are certain that it is Christ who is present here and grants us His body and blood. It is He who is causing by the word of His institution that the bread is His body and the cup is His blood. I say, this happens to those who believe because of His word and institution whether I eat worthily or unworthily.

Therefore, Christ cannot be absent from this institution, and therefore He cannot deceive His disciples, that is, those who believe that His word is true, so that He even permits wicked disciples to eat His body and drink His blood, lest you have any doubts about this sacred institution. Nothing departs here from the majesty of the body of Christ. Furthermore, nothing would depart from the majesty of the body of Christ, if the word of Christ which says: "This is My body; this is My blood" were found to be a lie because of wicked disciples.

As this body suffers nothing when a good person eats it, so this body suffers nothing if a wicked one eats it. However, the former uses that good body of Christ for his salvation, but the latter for his damnation, as Paul says [1 Cor. 12:29], just as God makes His sun rise upon the good and the evil, upon the grateful and the thankless, yet nothing departs from the glory of the sun. The institution of God does not perish by which He instituted that the sun rise every day, and that with His presence He restore a brighter day. Both thankful and thankless people ate the manna, and both good and evil people drank from the rock because of the Word of

God: "Each of you, go out and gather, etc."; and: "All your people and flocks will drink."

However, someone says: "Are you comparing the majesty of the body of Christ to these things?" I respond: "No." Instead, I am comparing the Word of God to the Word of God. As that Word wanted these things, so also it wants us to eat the body of Christ and to drink the blood of Christ according to the institution of Christ. The Lord does not rejoice about the betrayer who receives His body and blood in the Supper, but He does rejoice over the truthfulness of His Word. Because of the betrayer, the eternal Truth cannot will that what it says is not the truth: "This is My body. This is My blood."

Therefore, the wicked person takes and eats, but he does not do as Christ instituted "in remembrance of Christ," unless that perhaps is a hypocritical and pretended commemoration. After all, he does not trust in the death of Christ, as today the world is filled with the abominations of the Masses, in which the papists neither seek nor preserve the institution of Christ (as we said earlier), but many are seeking only this which Judas was looking for.

Although I am not concerned for those who hate the Gospel and pursue what they make out of the Sacraments of Christ, I merely comfort with these words those who before this were unknowing and communed with those and after this perhaps fell upon the ministers of the Church who they later detected were the associates of Judas. I comfort them that they not entertain doubts about the truthfulness of Christ's Word which they believe, as if, because of the wickedness of the minister, you are not receiving what you believe you are receiving according to the word of Christ. Here Christ, whose Word you hear and whose institution you believe, is giving you His body.

Also, Paul certainly wanted this when he repeated Christ's institution with the following words: "I received from the Lord what

I have handed over to you, that, on the night when He was betrayed, the Lord took bread, etc." [1 Cor. 11:23]. For this reason, Paul calls this "the bread of the Lord" and "the cup of the Lord," namely, which the Lord is consecrating with His words and which He Himself is giving us to show the truthfulness of His institution.

Otherwise we would have nothing else here than bread and wine, just as those Sacramentarians clearly have nothing else, because they do not believe that the bread of the Lord is the body of Christ and that the cup of the Lord is Christ's blood. What they don't believe they don't have in their entire participation. Therefore, they are without peril of becoming guilty of the body and blood of Christ in this Sacrament, lest anyone think that they have obtained no profit from so wonderful a teaching. However, the wicked disciples of Christ generally fall into this danger, for the Lord sometimes scolds and passes judgment on those for this reason that they not be condemned along with the whole world.

However, there are those who are corrupters and deniers of the Word and institution of Christ, and not only draw themselves away from Christ but also snatch up many others along with themselves into a headlong dive into error. Therefore, unless they repent when they have been admonished, they are unworthy of being people whom the Lord rebukes that they not be damned along with the whole world. Therefore, they must flee the coming wrath, for their problem is being against the word of Christ which remains forever while they perish.

They should know that Christ Himself here is giving us *His* body and blood (and not those of a fornicator) and that the bread and cup here are not of some holy human but of our Lord Jesus Christ, the Author of all holiness. They should know that this is not a supper of the Capernaites nor of Thyestes (O, what a terrible blasphemy!). Rather, it is the Supper of Him through whom all things are made alive, who is our Lord Jesus Christ, the God who is the Arranger of this sacred feast and is blessed forever. Amen.

Therefore, receive in a few words all the things which I have said; namely, that the bread of the Lord be for you His body. Believe His words and institution that you may eat worthily. Have confidence in His death, and you have responded to this sacred institution.

When we know these things about this institution of Christ by which it happens that the body of Christ cannot help but be present here, I am not disputing about the word of the consecration which they commonly call the consecration of the body and blood of Christ when they say that the ministers are consecrating the body and blood of Christ on the altar, provided that they attribute all these things here to the words and institution of Christ. We must arrogate nothing for ourselves beside the ministry which the Spirit has entrusted to us that we see to it that that which Christ instituted happens; namely, that the faithful eat and drink this Sacrament in remembrance of Christ.

Of what importance is it to battle about the words when we are agreed about the actual subject thereof? I know that Christ spoke His institution better than we speak our consecration, but I am not arguing about that. Where the bread is the body of Christ and the cup is the blood of Christ because of the institution of Christ, there the consecration of God, the consecration of the Holy Spirit, and the consecration of Christ are present. If we were able to speak only our own consecration and not that of Christ, we would be caving in to the Sacramentarians. However, when this consecration of God and Christ is present according to the word of Christ, who says: "This is My body. This is My blood," and that this institution has been instituted and given to us; I am not forbidding it if someone of the ministers may have spoken the consecration, just as our fathers also said it at times.

We repeat the institution of Christ over the bread and wine taken in this sacred use it in the presence of those who intend to commune so that they may hear and understand what they here must do and believe on the basis of Christ's words to eat the bread of the Lord and drink the cup of the Lord in remembrance of Christ, and that they may believe that the bread which they eat is the body of Christ and the cup which they drink is the blood of Christ. When we speak the institution of Christ over the bread and wine, we are embracing with our heart and loving with thanksgiving the institution of Christ and therefore are believing that what Christ says there (namely, that the bread is His body and the cup His blood) is true and we are doing what He Himself instituted that we do; namely, that we eat the body of Christ and drink His blood in remembrance of Him.

What we believe there on the basis of the word of Christ we have. If, then, someone shall have spoken our consecration because of his ministry, I shall permit this, provided no one say because of this manner of speaking that we are presuming that we—and not rather the Word and institution of Christ recited before those who intend to commune—are 'causing' the bread to be the body of Christ. That, you see, happens as a privilege and gift or benefit of our Ruler, Christ; for the institution of Christ does not demand that we make His body, but that we believe that this bread is the body of Christ. The person who does not believe this is faithless and makes Christ a liar in this institution.

As a result, we have the power to take and eat the body of Christ and to take and drink the blood of Christ truly in this Sacrament. Therefore the ministers of the Church who announce the word of salvation have the power also to give to others the bread of the Lord, about which He himself says: "This is My body," and the cup of the Lord, about which He Himself says: "This is My blood," namely, as He Himself causes His body and blood to be there; for these cannot be absent from His institution and the truthfulness of His word.

Paul expressed this power in this way, [1 Cor. 10:16]: "Is not the bread which we break the communion of the body of Christ?

And is not the cup of blessing which we bless the communion of the blood of Christ?" He does not say: "We break the bread, and the bread which we break or distribute in this way is because of the institution of Christ the communion or partaking of the body of Christ. And we bless the cup and the cup of blessing or the blessed cup which we bless for someone (not by which we are blessed, as someone of the Sacramentarians dares to corrupt this) is the communion or partaking of the blood of Christ." By instituting this Sacrament, Christ is saying about it: "This is My blood," just as He says about the former: "This is My body." In the same epistle, in the chapter following [v. 24], Paul says that Christ said: "This is My body which is broken for you."

The breaking or distribution is the responsibility of the ministers who distribute in the name of Christ. The communing or partaking is the responsibility of all who are taking, for we take in common. That is, each person takes his part of the one bread which we break, and each drinks from the one wine or cup which we drink here. This is what communing or partaking is. This communing or partaking is the communing and partaking of the body and blood of Christ, of the former when you eat the bread of the Lord, and of the latter when you drink the cup or chalice of the Lord. This bread is His and not common bread; this cup is His and not a common cup, for He says about the former: "This is My body which is given or broken for you," and about the latter: "This is My blood which is, etc."

That you not have doubts because of those who corrupt this passage of Paul, Paul himself explains what he means by "communion" or "participation." He says [1 Cor. 10:17], "For we who are many are one bread, one body, because we are all partakers of that one bread."

Although we commonly hear between the lines here: "One bread," namely, "We are one bread"; just as it follows: "We who are many are one bread"; it is not a bad way of thinking if you should interpret this in a godly way as follows:"We are one bread just as we are one body, because we are of the one bread about which Christ declares:'This is My body, and all of us share it.'"Elsewhere in Holy Writ you will not find a statement similar to this, to wit:"We who are many are one bread," but we often read:"We are one body."

It is of little importance to us as to who may by happy with this meaning, provided he be far from a corrupter of Paul's statement; for, whether we be one bread or one body, as Paul says, we all are partaking or communing of the one bread which we break, about which Christ says:"This is My body." Thus, you must see the same communion which I wanted to indicate that is in his godly statement as it has been commonly accepted.

Paul says:"We partake or commune of the one body which we break," about which Christ says: "This is My body." Paul says: "The bread which we break is the communion or partaking of the body of Christ." Paul is not saying here that we who are one bread and one body are eating ourselves mutually, as they now dare corrupt also this passage. In whatever way you may also understand that we are one bread, nevertheless he says that we are one bread and one body not because we are eating ourselves mutually, but because we all partake or commune of the one bread which we break.

Therefore, He is saying that the communion or participation which he had said was that of the body of Christ is the same as the communion or participation of the one bread, namely, of that which we break, about which Paul tells us Christ said:"This is My body which is broken for you," about which Paul also says:"He took the bread and, when He had given thanks, He broke it, etc."

Finally, shouldn't you finally see that the bread which we break and eat according to the institution of Christ is, as it is a partaking of the bread, so also it is the partaking and communing of the body of Christ; and that this bread of which we partake or commune is the bread of the Lord, distributed to many, and is the partaking or communing of the body of Christ?

Just as you have understood the communion of the body of Christ, so you will understand the communion of the blood of Christ, when Paul says: "Is not the cup of blessing which we bless the communion of the body of Christ," just as he also says elsewhere [2 Cor. 13:14] that "it is the communion of the Holy Spirit"?

I say, we are permitted to interpret in this way commonly, as if Paul is saying that we are one bread in the same way as we are one body. This is indeed a godly statement, as I have said; yet, to one who looks into the habit of Scripture more intensely, which is not in the habit of calling us "one bread," and into the context and way of thinking of this passage, it appears clearer than light that Paul is not speaking in this passage about an allegorical bread, as if we be one bread when we read: "For…one bread," but about the true bread about which he had said: "The bread which we break…," as when this was also said in the Greek without a verb: "For…one bread." There we must read between the lines: "For there *is* one bread," not: "…*we are* one bread."

He also wants to explain what he has called "the communion of the body of Christ" in these words: "Is not the bread which we break the communion of the body of Christ?" Why is that bread the communion of the body of Christ? Because, as he says: "There is one bread," namely, the bread which we break or distribute which God consecrated and gave to us with these words: "This is My body which is broken for you, for we who are many are one body," that is, all of us are members one of another under one Head who is Christ, at least according to our judgment. In the meantime, when we are all boasting about our faith in Christ and our one Lord Jesus Christ, we all want to be called "Christian" or to be considered a Christian, so that in the meantime I am not saying what Paul does not say: "Although we are many, we are all the one body of

Christ," but simply: "We, being many, are one body," that is, a single congregation. Therefore, let us not divide ourselves by sacrificing to idols, something which Paul deals with in this passage. You see, it is unworthy that we commune or become partakers of the table of the Lord Christ and of the table of devils. At the table of the Lord, we take the bread which is the body of Christ. At the table of devils we take not evil food but food which has been sacrificed to devils to the offense of our weaker brothers and with the opinion of being heathen as if by that eating we worship idols, which is a denial of Christ which we do not with words but by our very act. This is also an obvious fellowship with idolatry, regardless of how you may feel privately. But why are we who are many one body? Paul says: "Because we all partake of the one bread which we break about which Christ says: 'This is My body which is broken for you.'"

The many members, that is, all the members of one body, are one body (that you not be offended that he said "many" and "all"), because all members are enlivened from one bread and food, and because all members are sharers in the eating of one food. If any member has become dried up and dead from not benefiting from any food; nevertheless the food is good, and the person eats it on behalf of that member as well as for the other members. We judge that that member belongs to the body and is favored with the hope of restoration that the same food has the power to benefit it as it benefits others, until that member be cut off. It can also happen that the food it receives may harm a wounded member which otherwise would be healed by the same healing process. As a result, physicians forbid pork for people with an injured leg or injury elsewhere or are doing poorly for some other reason. Otherwise, those same physicians assert that pork nourishes well and befits the human nature quite well.

Who does not see to what this comparison pertains that I now may refrain from explaining it? If there is something which does not fit our subject, whosoever wishes may throw out whatever is my idea that that which Christ instituted in this very sacred Sacrament may remain whole. After all, we are arguing not in favor of *our* words but for the truthfulness of Christ's words.

Therefore, the communion of the body of Christ in this passage of Paul is that we all commune or partake of the one bread which we break, about which Christ says: "This"—or this bread—"is My body which is broken for you." Paul speaks in this way: "The bread which we break" (that is, which we distribute and which we make common to ourselves among ourselves when each takes his part) "isn't this the communion of the body of Christ?" Because there is one bread (namely, the one that we break), we do not give one bread to one, and another to another, but the same bread. "We who are many are one body." Why? Because from that one bread which we break we all, as members of one body, partake or commune. However, that bread which we break is that about which Christ says: "This is My body which is broken for you." Therefore, it is absolutely certain this is the communion of Christ's body of which Paul has spoken, by which the body of Christ is communicated to us, for Paul says: "We all partake of one bread"; and the institution of Christ says: "This one bread from which we all partake or commune is the body of Christ."

Paul certainly could have expressed this same address differently, namely, even in this way: "The breaking of bread is the breaking of the body of Christ." Why wouldn't he speak in this way, inasmuch as he later narrates the institution of Christ in these words: "…He broke it and said: 'This is My body which is broken for you.'"? In Scripture "to break bread" means to distribute or give bread, as you see in this passage of Isaiah [58:3]: "Break your bread for the hungry, etc."; and in the Lamentations of Jeremiah [4:4]: "The little children have asked for bread, and there was no one to break it for them." Or Paul could have spoken in this way: "The communion of bread or the bread with which we commune, is it not the communion of the body of Christ?"

We shall now declare these words more roughly against those who here make out of "the communion of the body of Christ" an invisible and spiritual communion by which believers and those acceptable to God are one before God in Christ and are truly in the body of Christ, something which God alone knows. After all, God knows those who are His. No one denies this communion of the faithful. In this passage, however, Paul speaks about it in the following words: "Is this not the communion of the body of Christ?" However, those people claim against the clear words merely this: that they do not permit the bread of the Lord to be the body of our Lord Jesus Christ according to the institution of Christ, for they see and perceive that Paul in this passage is perhaps hurling his spear against the wicked and presumptuous opinion of those and, when they cannot suffer the light of the sun, they try to obscure it if they can.

As a result, they even go on here to make out of the communion of the blood of Christ not a communion by which the blood of Christ is communicated to us or by which we drink commonly among ourselves the blood of Christ when we all drink from the cup about which Christ declared: "Drink of this, all of you; this is My blood, etc." Rather, they make out of it that same invisible communion about which we spoke, and they add that in this way we who are in Christ are called "one blood in Christ," just as we are called "one body in Christ." However, Scripture certainly is not speaking in this way here. Therefore, I would not resist if someone, in discussing in a godly way the mystic body of Christ, would say that we are one blood in Christ, or one cup, and even one wine. However, when they say these things here against the clear words of Paul and to deny the very clear institution of Christ, godliness and the Christian religion compel us to confess that this is a lie of Satan, the father of all lies.

Therefore, that communion is visible by which we all in common receive the visible Sacraments of Christ which are invisibly that which Christ institutes with His Word, because of which we all have received the Sacraments visibly, that is, we who are many are said to be, and are, one body. We are, I say, the sort of body not which God recognizes in all its members but such as we recognize, that is, the visible Church which we recognize from her confession of faith and fruits of love. In this Church, we consider those as good and through Christ they actually are good, unless they deceive us with lying hypocrisy. Although these may have sinned either against the faith or against love, nevertheless, they do come to their senses, acknowledge their error, and promise better things.

In this visible or, rather, external Church (which is not visible to the world but to us and is among us), that is, in this external body of Christ, so to speak, or congregation of all who are the members of Christ and who are considered as members of Christ, it can happen (But fortunate is that body or Church where this does not happen!) that someone is in our judgment a member of Christ. In the meantime, he is one body with us and in the one body of our Church but not in the public judgment of our Church because of his unsound teaching or because of causing offense because he is unwilling to accept correction. Thus he becomes condemned so that he is to us according to the teaching of Christ not a brother but a heathen and a publican, who in the presence of God is not a member of Christ but of Satan.

Therefore, we are one body among ourselves, while in the meantime, the Church does not pass judgment about secret matters, and love is not suspicious until we test the spirits as to whether their teaching is from God or until we see the public offenses of our brothers. You see, out first concern will be to save our erring brothers; then, if we cannot accomplish this, we cut them off from our body lest they harm the sincere part.

We do not excommunicate these from the fellowship of Christ or from the body of Christ unless (as I have said) by the external or public judgment of our Church we declare to our brothers that, because such people are unwilling to receive correction that they now have been excommunicated and do not belong to the body of Christ before God. The Church cannot truly excommunicate anyone unless he has first been excommunicated before God. We must excommunicate him once he has been convicted of teaching contrary to the faith of Christ or for being an offense to the Gospel of God, and is unwilling to accept correction. This we must do according to our judgment which God certainly approves of in heaven according to those words: "Whatsoever you have bound on earth, etc." [Mat. 16:19] Let such a person begin to fear the judgment of God (which he has despised), and let the rest approve of our judgment and in their terror be careful that they themselves not commit similar activities.

Until that time, however, we are not permitted to pass such judgment nor separate the weeds. We therefore often foster in our bosom disciples of Lucian and other despisers of God who, because they are with us in the one body of our Church, use the common Sacraments with us (although to their judgment, as Paul says, and not to their salvation). In fact, because they use our Sacraments, we cannot deny that they are one body with us, for we do not know anything which God denies more greatly, and He is the Knower of hearts, something which Paul has expressed in this way: "We who are many are one body because we all partake of the one bread."

If you ask for an example, take again that very crass example of the betrayer Judas. He, along with the apostles and other disciples of Christ, at that time was one body of the Church, for the apostles did not know another body. Therefore, they were not permitted to pass any judgment about it, just as they now are not permitted to pass judgments about such secret matters. Judas himself didn't want to be judged as such a person and therefore shared the same Sacraments with them. Furthermore, who would have presumed to judge anything when Christ Himself dignified him with the apostolic duty? He nevertheless in the sight of God did not belong to that body of the children of God who are truly the body and Church of Christ. Rather, he was a betrayer and a devil, just as Christ said, John 6[:70]: "Did I not choose twelve of you and one of you is a devil?"

Such a body or congregation of our Church is external, that is, we can recognize that about which Paul says: "We who are many are one body, because we all partake or commune of one bread." Otherwise he would not say later that "some eat and drink unworthily to their judgment." Also, in the assembly of the Corinthians, when they gathered together for the Lord's Sacraments, there were schisms and heresies, not to mention other offenses and not to say that some of them kept denying the resurrection of the flesh. Also, in 2 Corinthians he says that some were guilty of contentions, rivalries, disparaging remarks, arrogance, revolts, who were not sorry for their uncleanness, lust, and shamelessness.

And who does not also see in this passage that he feels badly about some people when he says: "I should not want you to be partners or fellows of devils. You cannot drink the cup of the Lord and the cup of devils; you cannot be sharers of the table of the Lord and of the table of devils. Do we provoke the Lord? Are we stronger than He?" [1 Cor. 10:20–21]

And yet, in the meantime, because all these had not been excommunicated by the public judgment of their Church, they were one body with the others, because they were not prohibited from the common Sacraments of Christ, just as he says here: "We who are many are one body," regardless of what sort of people they might be in the sight of God, "for we all partake of one bread." We people of Wittenberg are preserving this excommunication that we do not admit the guilty to the Sacraments of Christ, which is, as you see here, the ancient custom of the Church of Christ.

Scripture also is in the habit of speaking about the body and the Church in this way as sometimes visible; namely, as when it speaks about the body of the Church as we can perceive her. Thus you read that all offenses as well as all those who do iniquity are going to be collected from the kingdom of Christ at some time through the angels. You hear "kingdom of Christ" or "body of the Church," and yet you also hear of offenses and workers of iniquity, about which you read in Matt 7[:23]: "Depart from Me, etc." In John [15:2 and 6], Christ says: "He will remove in Me every branch which does not produce fruit... If anyone does not remain in Me, he will be sent out, etc." You hear "branch on the vine" as if a member of Christ and yet you hear nothing of drawing fertility from the vine, that is, nothing of receiving the Spirit from Christ, which branch the Father, as the Farmer, will take away, etc. For this reason, John is not speaking about the common disciples of the Gospel, but about those who are beginning to be teachers against the sound doctrine of Christ, as our sectarians are now. He says [1.2:19–20]: "They have come from us, but they were not of us. For, had they been of us, they surely would have remained with us, but [they left] that they may become obvious as people who are not all from us." As Paul says elsewhere: "Their foolishness will become known to all people." As we read in the Psalm [1:5]: "The wicked will not remain in the judgment nor sinners in the council of the righteous."

And what need is there to discuss this at length when Paul also speaks in this way about the body of the Corinthians or the Corinthian Church: "There must be heresies among you that those who have been approved may become manifest among you" [1 Cor. 11:19]? From these you see easily, as I spoke earlier, what Paul is discussing here; namely, that all they who are in the habit of attending the table of Christ not go to the table of devils lest those who

partake or commune of the bread and cup of the Lord (which is
the partaking or communion of His body and blood) become also
partakers of devils by eating and drinking among the worshippers
of idol-sacrifices which are sacrificed to idols. In this way, they leave
these very sacred ceremonies of Christ, that is, the external worship
of Christ which He Himself instituted in remembrance of Himself,
where we believe and do all the things which He Himself said and
commanded, and, in addition, where we do or believe nothing else
but what the institution of Christ has prescribed to us. As I say,
Paul is dealing with this subject: that the Corinthians themselves
see that they not abandon these ceremonies of the Lord for those
very wicked ceremonies of the heathen with which they worship
idols and profane the sacred mysteries of Christ which He handed over to His disciples for them to eat and drink with the same
mouth by which they [the Corinthians] have received the profane
sacraments of the heathen.

They are one body because they all are partaking of the
one bread of Christ which we break among ourselves. That is the
partaking of the body of Christ about which Christ says: "This is
My body which is broken for you." They are all members of the one
body just as all the members of a body naturally eat of one food.
Let them contain themselves within this body and one congregation and not be divided over idols. Let them fear the Lord Christ,
whom it is not safe to provoke, for we are not stronger than He.

However, here they are excusing themselves and say: "Actually,
Paul, what does this have to do with our knowledge and therefore
our conscience? We flee the worship of idols. Although we may sit at
the table of idols along with the heathen and eat of their food; nevertheless, we are not worshipping idols nor are we eating or drinking
the things they have sacrificed to idols. Our hearts are free because we
have a conscience that an idol is nothing in the world, nor is food or
drink taken there anything other than a good creation of God."

"Our friends, neighbors, and fellow-citizens (as a favor to whom we eat those things with them) otherwise would begin to hate and persecute us because of our own fault as people who are abandoning them over a completely empty matter. How, then, would we be worshipping idols which we know are nothing? How would food or drink—which we know is a good creation of God—be harmful? We are only running away from unsuitable things which would occur to us among heathen, if we are of no service to them in these matters. We are not on that account partakers of a wicked burnt offering because we eat of it. After all, we know that this food is nothing other than a good creation of God, even if a million heathen in their empty foolishness may have sacrificed it to idols. God has given us that food for us to receive with thanksgiving, not to heathen for sacrificing, etc."

To those who are in this way abusing their Christian freedom, Paul responds in this way what you read in the same epistle, c. 8[:4], and here, where he says: "You are correct when you say that an idol is nothing and that that sacrificing is useless. Nevertheless, you are not ignorant of the fact that when the heathen sacrifice they are not sacrificing to God but to devils. You are present at that worship, you don't speak against it but approve it by your very presence. You are preparing a fearful ruin here for weaker Christians whom you offend with this activity, for Christ died for them, too."

"In addition, what can the heathen feel about you in the meantime, other than that you worship idols along with them, although they may know that you also have some other God—Christ—something which they allow; namely, that individuals have their individual gods? How are you not partakers or sharers of idols and therefore of demons, when you participate or share, that is, when you eat and drink with others in a public place of idolatry, what they have sacrificed to devils—something of which you are not ignorant?"

See Israel according to the flesh! Aren't those who are eating the sacrifices of the Law offered to the true God according to the prescript of the Law as formerly or according to the Judaic opinion as now after the revelation of the Gospel, —I say, aren't they partakers of the altar of the Lord God, despite the fact that that may be temporary? Therefore those who are partakers or sharers of sacrificial victims (that is, those who eat those victims) are partakers and worshippers of that god who there is worshipped temporarily in some way or another.

So then, those who are partakers or sharers of those victims which are sacrificed to idols—no, to devils—that is, those who eat those things with other idolaters in a public place of idolatry and with the worship of idols, are partakers and sharers, too, of that public worship of devils and therefore of the devils themselves. No one, neither of the godly nor of the wicked, can feel differently about those, and they themselves by this public act confess and confirm this, however much they may in the meantime laugh in their hearts at such things and know that that is nothing. What they themselves are doing there, nevertheless, is *not* nothing. They are misleading others with their very offense, or at least are offending them. By their action, they are denying Christ and have become sharers of those things which were sacrificed to idols. In this way, they have become the partners and public sharers of demons, as they abandon and separate themselves from that one body in which they were in the habit of partaking of the one bread of Christ along with other Christians.

He says: "Furthermore, I should not want you to be sharers of devils. You may not drink the cup of the Lord and, at the same time, the cup of devils. You may not be partakers of the table of the Lord and of the table of demons. Partakers of demons are those who eat and drink the sacrificial victims of devils." I am spending no time over the fact that some laugh in secret at a wicked superstition, while in the meantime they mingle with those people, for Christ says, [Luke 12:9]:"He who has denied me before people, etc.," whatever he may feel in his heart in the meantime. Formerly, there were partakers in the Law of Moses who used to eat and drink the victims sacrificed to God, as it was said to the priests and Levites in Deu. 18[:1–2]:"The priests and Levites and all who are of the same tribe will have no part or inheritance with the rest of the people of Israel, because they will eat the sacrifices of the Lord and His offerings, and they will receive nothing from the possession of their brothers, for the Lord Himself is their inheritance, just as He Himself spoke to them." Also, there were other Israelites who would eat part of their voluntary offerings, and thus they became partakers of God when they ate what they had offered to God.

However, those are partakers of Christ who commune or partake of the things which Christ has instituted, that is, who eat not the common bread but the bread of the Lord Christ about which He says:"This is My body," and who drink not the common cup but the cup of the Lord Christ, about which He Himself says: "This is My blood, etc." This is the communion of the body and blood of Christ because of which we are partakers of Christ, for we are partakers or sharers by eating and drinking of those things which belong to Christ and which He Himself instituted, just as those are partakers of devils because by eating and drinking they become partakers or sharers of the things which were offered to devils.

Therefore, who does not see in this passage that the communion of the body and blood of Christ is external in which we eat and partake commonly of the body of Christ, when we break and eat the bread of Christ, about which bread He Himself says: "This is My body which is broken for you," and in which we commonly drink the blood of Christ when we drink the cup of blessing which we bless, about which He Himself says:"This cup is the new testament in My blood, etc.?" You see, He says: "This very external bread which we external ministers or which we external Christians break or distribute externally among ourselves or which we share externally among ourselves to eat externally but in commemoration of Christ (We need to use such crass language against those who in this passage are very spiritually spiritual for this reason alone: That they may deny what Christ instituted with very certain words; namely, that the bread of Christ which we break and eat is the body of Christ); —I say, is not the very bread which we break the communion or breaking or distribution of Christ, because the bread which we break is one? We who are many among us are one body and one Christian congregation, regardless of the fact that some are this in secret in the sight of God, because all of us partake of the one bread which we break, which partaking or communion of the one bread which we break is the partaking or communion of the body of Christ, because Christ also says clearly about the bread which we break: 'This is My body which is broken for you.'"

However, the partaking of the bread is external and, therefore, the partaking of the body of Christ here is also external because (as we see from the words of Paul) these two are the same in the Lord's Supper according to His institution. The bread is the body of Christ; therefore, the communion of the bread is the communion of the body of Christ. The cup which we bless is the blood of Christ; therefore, the communion of the cup is the communion of the blood of Christ.

Here it can happen just as said earlier, that someone may partake with us in this sacred remembrance of Christ with the body and blood of the Lord in the external partaking; that is, he may eat along with us in the one congregation or body of our Church the bread which, because of the institution of Christ is the body of Christ and drink the cup which because of the institution of Christ is the blood of Christ. In the meantime, however, he does not partake with us in the internal partaking by which the faithful before God are one spiritual body in Christ (as you read in John 17) and he is not a member of Christ (just as happened in that body of the apostles and disciples of Christ, when Judas the Betrayer of the Lord, along with the others, received the holy Sacrament of Christ, as we read in the Gospel of Luke) or may be a member of Christ by predestination. Nevertheless, he may now not have an internal communion with us because of a present fault, but, by the goodness of God, he is invited to repent. In the meantime, he does not desire to receive correction, although he may be in the body of our Church. That is, he has not been excommunicated from us by the manifest judgment of the Church. He is also unworthy of that external communion of which we are now speaking, even if he partake, that is, even if he eat with us the bread which is the body of Christ and drink the cup which is the blood of Christ.

After all, Christ cannot deny the reality of His institution because of human malice, but where the reality of this institution does not exist (as is the case among our Sacramentarians) it is not strange if the things which Christ instituted are not there. Take away the institution of Christ, and the bread is bread, the wine is wine. Where people have preserved the institution of Christ and believe it, there the things which Christ instituted truly exist. If some people do not receive well the body and blood of the Lord in this Sacrament of the bread and wine, we must not on that account accuse Him who instituted it nor must we deny the things which He instituted.

However, we should not be afraid that the body suffer anything in this sacred mystery, because God also makes His sun rise upon the good and the evil, on the gold and dung. On that account, we must not accuse the Creator of the sun who arranged that the sun rise in this way, nor should we deny that the sun is the sun, for the sun mixes itself with its brightness, heat, glory, and effect with the dung, or certainly permits the dung to take up the gold and causes it to stink worse for the time of an age. Because the fault lies in the dung and, in the meantime, because nothing departs from the glory of the sun, we must give thanks to God for giving the blessing of the sun to creatures under heaven for their safety and that He doesn't take it away because of the stinking sewer. This is not something we must feel against this sacred institution, because even the unworthy receive the Sacraments of Christ. Rather, we must give thanks for such a great regard which permits the unworthy disciples to receive these Sacraments and us to become uncertain about His institution which He expressed with such certain words.

The most holy Institutor, Christ, instituted for us a most sacred religious ceremony to which no human ceremonies can be compared, that we who come to this sacred ritual which Christ has prescribed to us may eat the bread of Christ which is His body and drink the cup which is His blood as often as we wish until He come, that is, all the way up to the last day, in remembrance of Him, that is, as we preach both publicly and mutually among ourselves the benefits of the death of Christ. Paul interprets that in this way and says: "As often as you eat this bread and drink this cup, you announce the Lord's death until He come." [1 Cor. 11:26]

Meanwhile the "Mass-masters" are making out of so sacred a ritual a marketing device or something other than what Christ prescribed, and they forbid the laity from what He instituted. They are no longer yielding to the revealed truth. They will have seen or certainly will see when Christ will have appeared that it is a terrible thing that such sacred things which He instituted could have reached so great a profanation and abomination. They make out of the Sacrament what Christ did not institute, they prohibit what He commanded, which is the height of abominations, worthy to be removed only by the judgment of the Last Day, for dogs, dissatisfied as they are, don't know how to blush.

In fact, our Sacramentarians—although some do this in one way and others in another way—are taking away from us this most sacred ceremony which Christ instituted, denying as they do that the bread which we eat according to the institution of Christ is the body of Christ and that the cup is His blood. Then, when we press them hard, they make the same Sacrament uncertain, if we are willing to follow them. You see, they say: "Christians and believing Christians—in fact, correctly-believing Christians—eat there the true body of Christ and drink the true blood of Christ in the living Word of God through true faith." However, I shall speak about these points at the end.

Therefore, there is no doubt that the communion of the body of Christ in this Pauline passage is not that spiritual one by which only those commune who commune worthily or who are always believers (as I shall say later from John 6) or who receive this Sacrament as many times as they may have wanted in the congregation of our Church (in which we who are many are one body). Rather, it is that communion which they call "sacramental," by which by the power of the words and institution of Christ, who orders us to eat there the bread which He Himself says is His body and to drink the cup which He Himself says is blood. In this communion, we truly and not in a feigned way receive the body of Christ in the bread and the blood of Christ in the cup, and all of us receive it in our own body, that is, in our congregation, whether they are worthy or unworthy.

You see, Paul is saying that the bread which we break is this about which we say is the communion of the body of Christ and the cup which we bless is the communion of the blood of Christ. In addition, he says that we who are many are one body because we all partake or commune of that one bread which we break, which is the communion of the body of Christ, about which Christ says: "This is My body which is broken for you." This we do either worthily or unworthily, just as Paul says in the following chapter, that some eat and drink unworthily to their damnation. Certainly in this passage Paul is saying that those commune unworthily who go away from the table and cup of the Lord to the table and cup of devils, from the ceremonies of Christ to the ceremonies of Satan, from the body of our Christian Church or congregation to the congregation of the heathen, which is also that of Satan.

From these statements, you will also grasp in passing what I feel about the power of concomitance (as they call it). As far as the words of institution are concerned, the bread is the body of Christ and not the blood of Christ because Christ says: "The bread is My body." He does not say: "The bread is My blood," or: "The bread is Christ," or: "The bread is My body and My blood, and the whole thing that I am and the entire Trinity." Also, Paul says: "The bread which we break is the communion of the body of Christ." He does not say: "...of the body and blood of Christ"; or: "...of the whole Christ"; or: "...of the whole Trinity," because he is dividing the communion so that he says the one part is of bread, that is, of the body of Christ, and the other is of the cup, that is, of the blood of Christ. He does not mix those two together into one, just as the institution of Christ does not mix those two together nor want them to be mixed together, as the papists persuade their laity of that mixing together, contrary to the institution of Christ which commands that we drink of the cup.

So, too, as far as the words of institution are concerned, the cup is the blood of Christ and not the body of Christ, for Christ says: "The cup is My blood." He does not say: "The cup is My body," or: "The cup is Christ," or "the cup is My blood and My body and the whole of who I am, and the whole Trinity." Also, Paul says: "The cup of blessing which we bless is the communion of the blood of Christ." He does not say: "...of the blood and body of Christ," or: "... of the whole Christ," or: "...of the holy Trinity."

Christ also divides this Sacrament into eating and drinking. He commands us to eat the bread which He says is His body, and He orders us to drink the cup which He says is His blood. The papists, on the contrary, command that the cup not be drunk as Christ commands; but, just as they command against Christ, you must imagine that by eating the bread you are also drinking. For that reason, that foolish presumption and wicked tradition have advanced to the point that they are now compelled to place them ahead of the institution of Christ. Here their eating and drinking are the same thing, when the institution of Christ does not want them to be the same thing but orders that we eat and drink also externally.

No one should think that this is my opinion alone. The sophist theologians also have said it before we did; namely, that, as regards the words of Christ, who says:"This is My body. This is My blood," he who eats the body does not drink the blood, and he who drinks the blood does not eat the body.

This is the sacramental eating and drinking by which both the worthy and the unworthy eat and drink the body and blood of Christ. Here we must not follow human thoughts as to whether the wine can be the body of Christ without blood the way the body of a living cow cannot exist without blood, and whether the body is in the chalice; otherwise, we would call it not blood, but a blood stream. Those thoughts, you see, are empty and foolish and Christian faith does not follow them, but the words of Christ, as He says:"The bread is My body. The cup is My blood." The Christian faith sets aside all other thoughts and believes that the true body of Christ is present here in the bread and the true blood of Christ is in the cup. Or, that no one be falsely charged, it believes that this bread is the true body of Christ and the cup of the Lord is the true blood of Christ. Finally, it believes that Christ instituted these very things that both the worthy and unworthy receive them.

Christ wanted to institute the commemoration of His death. Therefore He commanded that we eat the bread which He declares is His body that we may remember or preach and teach among ourselves that His body was handed over into death on behalf of us. He also commanded us to drink the cup which He declares is His blood that we may remember or teach and preach that His blood was shed for us for the remission of our sins.

He instituted it that when that remembrance is made known among Christians, they do not listen to the pseudapostles and the "righteousness preachers" who preach that something else is necessary for salvation and the absolution or remission of sins than the body of Christ which was handed over for us and the blood that was shed for us for the remission of our sins.

However, when even now the papists have taken away the true use of this Sacrament from the Church as heretical and condemned as if that be heretical which Christ commanded and instituted; then all the sects of destruction have grown powerful and have taught what anyone wanted, while the righteousness of God through Jesus Christ (which is the true Gospel) has become only silent and finally even condemned. The person who knows well this institution of the Supper from the words of Christ also knows what the way of salvation and the remission of sins is.

Here, then, according to the words of Christ's institution, are the true body and true blood of Christ. The Christian faith cannot entertain doubts about the fact that Christ gave those for this use alone; namely, that we eat and drink them in remembrance of Christ and for no other use. Furthermore, I believe that no one can know how the body and blood of Christ are here, and no one should be concerned that he doesn't know it because we do not know this from the word of Christ, nor did He command us to know that. Christ commands only that we believe what He says here, and that we do what He Himself commands. This is a sufficient response to the institution of Christ.

Moreover, what the sophists say about concomitance in this Sacrament, especially of the bread which is the body of Christ, they seem to have invented to the harm of the institution of Christ; namely, that the laity not receive the cup of the Lord through concomitance; as they say, they receive the blood of the Lord in the bread. They themselves say this, but Christ says something else.

They call it "concomitance" and speak in this way. Although the body of Christ may be only in the bread according to the form of Christ's words; nevertheless, as a result of natural concomitance (because the body cannot be without blood), blood is also there. As a result of the same natural concomitance, the soul of Christ is also there. However, because the body, blood, and soul of Christ (that is, the humanity of Christ) has been so united with His divinity that they cannot be separated by the same concomitance, there is also present there the divinity of Christ and, at the same time, in the bread the whole Christ is also present—God and man. Furthermore, where the Son is, there are also the Father and the Holy Spirit. By the same natural concomitance, therefore, Christ and, at the same time, the whole Trinity are present in the bread. I am not mentioning what else they have said is contained in the bread by this reasoning because of which the Sacramentarians recently have been laughing at us by no merit nor fault of ours because they have placed this wicked verse in a certain pamphlet of Zwingli as if we must offer whatever each may have left. Therefore, they have called this "concomitance" in the bread, which they undoubtedly will also be compelled to do in the case of the cup or the wine.

Who has commanded us to teach such things? Natural and unnatural consequences and human thoughts mean nothing here. We must look only to the word of Christ. Whatever it says, this you must believe, say, and teach. Whatever it does not say, see to it that you have not spoken that, especially that you have not spoken it to the harm of the word of Christ, as has happened here, where, because of their concomitance, they have denied the chalice of the Lord to the laity, contrary to the word and institution of Christ, which not even an angel may change.

By the same reasoning, another sophist would deny us the bread and would say that it is enough if someone receive only the chalice because by natural concomitance he would have all things in the chalice, even that which Christ did not institute in the chalice. Thus, it would permit any fool to change the institution of Christ as he may wish and, as a result, do whatever he wished just as the papists have changed it. Although Christ says and commands: "Take and drink of this, all of you. This cup is the new testament in My blood, etc."; they say: "Don't take. Don't drink. This is a Hussite and Lutheran heresy. Even if you only wish to drink the chalice of the Lord, you will have taken the chalice at great peril to your faith. The fact that you want to drink the chalice that you may draw from it the blood of Christ is a sure sign that you do not believe that the body in the bread also has blood."

There is a bishop who recently commanded by public edict that all the pastors of his churches teach and indoctrinate the people as to what is contained under the bread. It also came into his mind that his people listen not to Christ but to a human fiction that under the bread is contained blood, and that they should not desire to follow Christ but the good intention of that holy bishop. Well, let that bishop teach whatever he wishes is contained in the bread— even heaven and earth. What does this have to do with Christians? Here, however, we are disputing with that bishop whether, when Christ says: "Take and drink the cup which is My blood," he [the bishop] may forbid it and say: "Don't take and drink." Christ commands, the bishop forbids. To whom must we listen? However, the world is filled with these insanities.

Listen therefore, if you have not yet been listening. By instituting this Sacrament, Christ instituted the remembrance and announcement of His death, and therefore gave us to eat the bread, His body, and to drink the cup, His blood, in remembrance or announcement of His body handed over on the cross for us and of His blood shed for us for the remission of our sins. So certainly, then, did He hand over this body and this cup in this Sacrament to eat and drink so that even in the meantime some people in our body or in the congregation of our Church receive them unworthily to their judgment, having become guilty of the body and blood of the Lord. This is because the institution of the Lord and the Word of the Lord cannot be made a lie because of our wickedness, that, because of the wickedness of some, others not become doubters of the truthfulness of His institution. For the sake of the godly, our Lord Christ suffers this injury of the ungodly to His body and blood but in such a way that this happens in His Sacrament. Otherwise, He Himself suffers nothing, not when the worthy eat His body and drink His blood in the Sacrament nor when the unworthy eat and drink it.

Although the unworthy ought not eat the body and drink the blood of Christ in the Sacrament, nevertheless they can do this. But who may have permitted the unworthy to eat and drink the whole Christ and the whole Trinity? In addition to those things which Christ expressed in His institution, no one should assert anything here. If you don't grasp with your reason that the bread is the communion of the body of Christ and not of the blood and that the cup is the communion of the blood of Christ and not of the body, or if you prefer, that the bread is the body of Christ and not the blood of Christ and that the cup is the blood of Christ and not the body; then give glory to the institution of Christ, which says that the bread is His body and the cup is His blood, and which commands us to eat His body and drink His blood in remembrance of Christ. After all, are we to change—not to mention forbid— what Christ, the Lord of majesty, institutes and commands? Will dust and ashes do this and go unpunished?

But that I not appear to be casting out completely that concomitance, I make a distinction. To the unworthy, I attribute a sort of concomitance of sin and damnation, for if anyone sins against this Sacrament, he also sins against the whole Christ and the whole Trinity. To the worthy, however, I attribute a sort of concomitance of the glory of God and salvation, for if anyone communes worthily, in whatever part he has grasped Christ, whether in the Sacrament (provided he receive it as Christ instituted it) or with a spiritual eating outside the Sacrament, at the same time he will grasp the whole Christ and the whole Trinity according to those words: "He who loves Me will keep My word, and My Father will love him, and We shall come to him and make our dwelling place with him." [John 14:23] You will also take up this concomitance only when you receive some preacher of the Gospel of Christ, just as the apostle said: "He who receives you receives Me, and he who receives Me receives Him who sent Me." [Mat. 10:40]

However, why do they bring forth their 'concomitances' against the conduct of this Sacrament which the worthy and the unworthy receive? After all, neither angels nor men should make anything out of that procedure with their teachings than what Christ instituted. Let human presumption remain silent and give the glory to the word of Christ.

All these things which I have been saying concern that concomitance which people have dreamed up against the institution of Christ. You see, He did not say: "Drink the bread which is My blood; eat the cup which is My body"; or: "Eat and drink the bread which is at the same time My body and My blood." Rather, He commanded something far different, for He commanded that we eat the bread which is His body and drink the cup which is His blood. And who are you who think you must only eat but forbid the drinking? Do you condemn that as heretical? By what right? By what authority? It certainly is contrary to the word of Christ and comes from the teaching of the Antichrist. According to Paul, those are the doctrines of devils. I say, all these things which I have now said, —who does not see that they pertain to that external communion which occurs in the Sacrament of the body and blood of Christ, about which Paul says: "The bread which we break, etc.," although they may appear to be beside the point?

Already, for a long time now, I hear people objecting to us from this passage of Paul that the sacrifices made to idols which are not the actual devils substantially; and yet Paul says that those who eat are companions or partners of devils. Thus, neither the bread nor the wine in the Supper are the body and blood of Christ substantially and really, although Paul says: "The bread which we break is the communion of the body of Christ." They are throwing up to us these and similar inappropriate matters as if Paul is not explaining himself immediately when he says: "You cannot drink the cup of the Lord and the cup of devils; you cannot be partakers of the table of the Lord and of the table of devils." Partaking of the table of the Lord is partaking of the body of Christ. Partaking of the table of demons is partaking of sacrifices to idols. This latter is undoubtedly the partaking of devils, just as the former is the partaking of Christ. Satan is the author of the latter, just as Christ is of the former.

On the table of devils are the things which people have sacrificed to devils and not to God. At the table of Christ, Christ Himself breaks or distributes to us and sheds for our eating and drinking those things which He offered on the cross for us to His Father. Through His blood, He made us kings and priests for God the Father. Therefore, He Himself is the eternal Priest for we who are a holy priesthood, a chosen nation, and a priestly kingdom. He offers for us His sacrifices which He Himself as our Priest, Pacifier of God, and our Propitiation consecrated on the cross with His perfect sacrifice, that we may always be incorporated by faith to His body and blood, just as I shall say in my commentary on John 6, and just as often as we shall have wished we take them in our own body or in the congregation of our Church according to His institution. Nevertheless, we must see to it that no one partake unworthily in this Sacrament, for outside of this Sacrament no one can partake worthily.[6]

However, in whatever way you may have taken those matters, Paul certainly takes the partaking of the body of Christ in the Supper and the partaking of bread as the same thing. He says: "Isn't the bread which we break the communion or partaking of the body of Christ?"; and: "We all partake of the one bread which we break."

Moreover, if you are unwilling to hear here that we are dealing with nothing other than that we not be defiled by the worship of idols in our eating and drinking, and if you have begun to press hard according to the dreams of our own brain those who are in the habit of coming to the Lord's table as if all things must be similar at both tables, that of the Lord and that of devils—I say, if this is true, first, you will act contrary to the rationale of all comparisons in which it is not necessary that all things be corresponding, but only those things because of which we have taken them up. Next, Paul obviously resists you here and says that he does not want all things to be alike here, for, as he says: "An idol is nothing, and what has been sacrificed to idols is nothing." However, this is not something you can say about the bread and wine in the Supper, namely, that they are nothing, for it would be wicked to say that what Christ has instituted is nothing.

I believe that those false accusers who anxiously and risibly seek something with which to raise an objection to the manifest Word of God finally are going to compel us to admit that even the devils have said in that public worship about offerings to idols: "These are our bodies; this is our blood," just as we confess that Christ said: "This is My body; this is My blood," because, as they

---

6 Text reads "*indigne* - unworthily," but that seems to be an erratum.

say, all things here ought to be alike. The latter are wicked, the former are godly. You see here what foolish and risible things I could here object to those calumniators by right of their usage, were we free or permitted to be inappropriate in these serious matters.

It is Paul's way of thinking in that entire tenth chapter [of 1 Corinthians] that we neither provoke nor irritate the Lord lest that stronger One condemn us. Those provoke Him who despise Him when they go off to the worship of idols through that freedom by which they are otherwise permitted to eat all things. Those provoke Him who pursue their own lusts and shameful activities and become hardened against the Word of God. They are testing God and murmuring against the divine will, as the faithless Jews did in the wilderness. Those provoke God when they despise those things as if they are doing nothing against God and yet in the meantime boast that they are Christians and followers of the Gospel because they have listened to the Gospel, received the Sacraments of Christ, read Holy Writ, and are considered among the people of God, just as did those Jews who boasted that they were the children of Abraham, the people of God, whom the Lord had led out of Egypt through the Red Sea, had eaten the manna, drunk from the rock, etc.

Examples of their ruin have been written for us that we not perish in like manner if we begin to behave in the sight of God with contempt, for those are in a different situation who sin out of ignorance or weakness, who acknowledge their sin, repent sincerely, and demand pardon and a remedy from the Father through Jesus Christ our Lord.

This is the entire summary of that chapter. In the meantime, Paul frightens people away from the worship of idols with another argument, namely this: it is unworthy that those who are in the habit of coming to the table of the Lord should also come to the table of devils, from our body to the body of the heathen, from our unity to the scattering of those heathen and the mixing of Satan, etc.

EPILOG.

But we have now said enough with this little book of ours about our consecration; that is, how it happens that in the Supper we eat the bread or the body of Christ, and drink the cup or His blood; namely, on the basis of the institution of Christ, who commands that here we eat His body and drink His blood. He who ordered and instituted this cannot be absent from His institution, provided we believe here what He Himself says, namely, that the bread is His body which is broken for us and the cup is His blood which is shed for us for the remission of sins and we do what Himself commands, namely, that we eat and drink in remembrance of Him. This is the entire rationale of this Sacrament, and we are permitted to add nothing to it nor take anything from it by which to change that institution.

We accept these things from the words and institution of Christ. Matthew, Mark, Luke, and Paul wrote these things for us in clear and non-puzzling language. On the basis of their words, I also write in this way: "I have received from the Lord what I have also handed down to you, etc."

We are not hindering any minister of this Sacrament here, even if we should encounter some Judas. After all, the institution of Christ is not truthful because of the goodness of the minister nor is it a lie because of his wickedness. Christ gives us this Sacrament, and our faith receives it. Only those who deny that these things are here—contrary to the word of Christ—do not have here the body and blood of Christ.

That the body of Christ is present here for those who are eating and that His blood is present here for those who are drinking, it is enough to believe that Christ does not lie but speaks the truth when He says, "This is My body; this is My blood." Trust causes you to eat and drink worthily, for by it you believe that your remission of sins comes through the death of Christ and through the shedding of His blood. Now the body of Christ is also being broken for us at His table. See to it that you do not receive against yourself what it given to you here on behalf of yourself.

After this, they cannot raise the objection against us that fornicators, adulterers, usurers, and others make up for us the body of Christ because we say that the saints, the chaste, and the godly make the body of Christ for us. With His institution, Christ orders and institutes that we eat His body and drink His blood believing that the bread which we eat according to His institution is His body because He says: "This bread which I am ordering you to eat is My body," and that the cup which we are drinking is His blood because He says: "This cup from which I command all of you to drink is My blood." Paul also says: "Is not the cup of blessing which we bless the communion of the blood of Christ? And is not the bread which we break the communion of the body of Christ?" Therefore it is not some man, some saint or some sinner, who makes here the body of Christ for us, for no one makes or consecrates what Christ here made and consecrated for us with His Word.

Someone may have said that we consecrate the Sacrament of the body and blood of Christ because of our ministry by which we pronounce the institution of Christ in the name of Christ as ministers of our Church in the congregation of those who intend to eat and drink and by which we commemorate the death of the Lord, as we preach our redemption and give the Sacrament. Should someone say this, he is speaking in a godly way, provided that in the meantime he attribute nothing to man beside the ministry, and provided that the minister preach Christ the Lord as the Institutor and Giver of this Sacrament. Because of His great love for us, it pleased

Him to offer His body and blood through which He redeemed us not only to be killed but also to be eaten and drunk in remembrance of His death. This He did in such a way that we not only can receive the Sacrament, but also receive it freely. Paul also expressed this ministry of ours when he said: "...which *we* bless," and "...which *we* break."

Moreover, as He does not take away the truthfulness of His institution because of unworthy ministers, so also He does not take it away because of unworthy eaters. Some people indeed eat and drink the body and blood of the Lord unworthily, something which Paul says. Christ speaks in this way in Luke [22:21] says: "The hand of him who is betraying Me is at the table." Mark [14:23] says: "They all drank of it," and in their number was undoubtedly Judas. Some of the ancient teachers write that Judas had not been present at that time but had left before, but the Gospel does not allow this as true; for, just as the manna from heaven and the water from the rock were common to the Jews, although most of them were not pleasing to God, so the bread which is the body of Christ and the cup which is the blood of Christ are common to us, both good and evil.

Christ wanted His Church to be so certain about this institution that He even permits the unworthy to eat and drink what He instituted that we entertain no doubts that those who are in our body, that is, in the assembly, eat and drink here the body and blood of Christ. Otherwise, this debate would have gone on forever: he eats the body of Christ, but perhaps he does not eat, because if he is worthy, he eats, but if he is not worthy, he doesn't eat, etc. This, however, is something Christ would never have instituted.

Furthermore, the unworthy eat the true body of Christ, something which they also believe because of the word of Christ, who says: "This bread is My body"; and they drink the true blood of Christ, which they believe is here because of the word of Christ, who says: "This cup is My blood." However, they are eating and drinking in the Sacrament, in this sacred mystery, where only the word of Christ causes the bread to be the body of Christ and the cup His blood for us, so that in the meantime, you have no suspicion because of your human thinking that the body and blood of Christ here are suffering something whether the worthy or the unworthy have eaten and drunk.

Here people will cry out: "If the Pomeranian were to understand here his own words, he would be denying along with us that this bread is the body of Christ, because he is saying: 'Here the body and blood of Christ are present and are eaten and drunk, but in the Sacrament.'" Although I am explaining sufficiently and more than sufficiently in words I have repeated often, nevertheless they are not hearing: "The ancient teachers spoke in this way." Nevertheless, those teachers did not deny that the bread of the Lord is His body and the cup His blood. So, too, we are speaking as has been our custom up to this point. If the words of the ancients or if our own words should displease you, and if you should not allow us to use the word "Sacrament" and others, then throw out the words of the ancients and throw out ours, too, provided you leave whole for us the words of Christ on the basis of which both the ancients and we said that the bread of the Lord is His body and the cup His blood.

After all, our struggle here does not involve human words (whether they are those of the ancients or our own words), but the word of Christ, without which I would happily allow that the bread is nothing else but bread. However, if something in the words of the ancients or in our words should have offended you as a result of which one could deny either by calumny or even truly that in the Supper of Christ the bread is not His body and the cup is not His blood, then let the human words be destroyed and become nothing that the truthfulness of the institution of Christ not be denied through those words. No authority in the Church should prevail against the word and authority of Christ.

The ancients said some things too broadly in this case, especially Augustine, because at that time there was no debate over this subject. The ancients nevertheless confessed in many very clear words in other places that both the worthy and the unworthy eat and drink the body and blood of the Lord in the Supper. Read all the ancients, and you will discover this!

Next, among the ancients that way of thinking was undoubted so that on the basis of the words of Christ's institution, the Catholics often were compelled to accept the arguments against themselves.

Already for a long time after the days of the apostles, Christians were often accused among the heathen of eating human flesh or the flesh of some infant in secret little gatherings and of sacrificing with human blood, something you read twice in the *Historia Ecclesiastica* and which you can see in Tertullian's *Apologeticum*. I do not doubt that this happened[7] because of the report of this Sacrament which those people celebrated, until even the apostate Averroës wrote: "There is no people in the world worse than Christian people, because they gobble up the God they worship, something which no other people have ever done."

I confess that here there is the true body of Christ, not an imaginary nor fictitious nor lying body, because Christ says: "This is My body," and that very body is eaten according to the institution and command of Christ. By the fact that I mention "Sacrament" and "mystery" (as do the ancients), I am signifying that the bread is indeed the true body of Christ and that we are truly eating it according to the word and institution of Christ. However, we do this invisibly, insensibly (if you not pay attention to the external Sacrament or to the bread and wine as signs, which are the body and blood of Christ), and incomprehensibly, so that we do not see

7 That is, that they were so falsely accused.

nor sense nor understand that the body of Christ is there except by faith in the word of Christ.

Otherwise, no sense grasps nor can any reason understand that the bread is the body of Christ and the cup His blood, and that both the worthy and unworthy can eat and drink it without inconvenience to the elements, and yet both have the institution of Christ. It is wicked not to believe this, for Christ says: "This is My body; this is My blood. Eat and drink. Don't be afraid that when you eat My body and drink My blood, they will perish. Nothing bad can happen to anyone unless that be brought on unworthily by those who eat and drink unworthily."

The word of Christ causes the body and blood of Christ to be here and us to be able to eat His body and drink His blood. We must have no doubts about this, for the word of Christ has expressed that this is the situation and that it happens and should happen in this way. How this is and how this happens properly without any impropriety to Himself no one can know or understand. Because all these things here depend on the word of Christ (something which no one should deny), no one can know them because Christ has not expressed this with His word.

Therefore, contrary to all the things which seem absurd to human reason, we must here give glory to the Word of God as we do in all the articles of faith. Here we understand all things when we believe all the things which Christ says and do all the things which He commands. Furthermore, by not believing, by not doing, and by not omitting, they are going to attempt something against the rationale of this institution. However, we say this only in passing against those who cry out against it.

The wickedness of the Sacramentarians denies and twists violently in a different direction that which Christ says: "This is My body; this is My blood." The wickedness of the papists changes what Christ ordained and instituted. It not only changes by doing something other than that, but even forbids and claims it is heretical. Christ commands that we eat and drink in remembrance of Him, but they order their people to sacrifice for the living and the dead, even if the puny priest alone eats and drinks and gives no one anything to eat and drink, regardless of what Christ said with His words: "Take, eat, all of you drink." With reference to the external cup, Christ commands and says: "Drink of this, all of you. This is My blood"; but they command that the laity not drink unless they wish to be damned heretics.

To those concomitance-claimers (that is, to those who with their concomitance with which they mix together human reason with the Word of God and confirm that wickedness which condemns and forbids what Christ commands, ordains, and institutes) we say: "Let them permit us this unharmed ordination and institution of Christ which neither angels nor men may change, and in the meantime, let them keep their own thoughts to themselves and leave the Word of God to us."

You see, we must confess that the unworthy also eat and drink this bread and cup of the Lord, that is, the body and blood of Christ in the Sacrament which Christ consecrated for us with His institution. However, we do deny that the unworthy eat and drink the whole Christ and the whole Trinity through that concomitance, because to eat and drink the whole Christ and the whole Trinity simultaneously is to be incorporated into Christ and united with God in reality. (We shall speak about this eating later in our commentary on John 6.)

However, we must not deny this, namely, that through concomitance, the person who receives here the Lord's body and blood unworthily not only becomes guilty of the Lord's body and blood but also of the whole Christ and of the whole Trinity and, therefore, is guilty of harming the majesty of God. We say this that our celebrators of the Mass may learn to fear the judgment of God and that all Christians may learn to respond to this sacred institution that they not teach anything at variance with it. Or, do we provoke the Lord? Are we stronger than He?

In addition, we confess that through concomitance the person who receives here the body and blood of Christ will become a partaker and partner of the whole Christ and of the whole holy Trinity not by force of the Sacrament, which is the body and blood of Christ, but by virtue of his worthy communion which comes of faith or trust in Christ.

If they were to teach *this* concomitance, they would take nothing from the sacred institution of Christ and, in fact, would be honoring it. However, it is a cursed doctrine having every human thought which does this under any guise of truth, so that it denies or changes—not to say damns and judges heretical—what Christ has commanded and instituted. Amen.

But now, after we have confirmed our teaching from the Word of God, why don't we also indicate with just a few words the godly people and teachers who once both sensed and taught the same doctrine, not because we depend upon human authority in matters of our faith, but that we may see that in this case those had the same way of thinking as do we from the same Word of God? For whatever they or we say without the Word of God or on the basis of the Word of God which we understand poorly, let that be nothing. Let it perish, for the truth of God remains forever.

What the blessed martyr Cyprian attributed excessively to ministers of the Church in favor of his re-baptizing, and what Jerome attributed elsewhere, we shall show quite clearly as they write in their commentaries on the [first] epistle to the Corinthians: "As the Word which we preach is not ours but that of God, so also the Sacraments which we must administer are not ours but of Christ who instituted and gave them."

This is something which Augustine confesses in these words, against the letter of Bishop Parmenianus, Bk. 2, c. 10: "Although all the Sacraments hinder those who handle them unworthily, nevertheless they are a blessing to those who receive them worthily, as the Word of God bears witness: 'Do what they say, but don't do what they do.' You see, although there are among Christians some bishops or ministers who are dead through their ungodly wickedness, nevertheless that one is alive about whom it is said: 'This is he who baptizes because Christ rose from the dead and now is not dead, etc.'" In c. 11, Augustine says: "When Parmenianus wished to prove that natural humans cannot produce spiritual children, he added testimony from the Gospel: 'That which is born of the flesh is flesh, and that which is born of the Spirit is spirit,' [John 3:6] as if we are saying that any human produces spiritual children through himself, and not through the Gospel, in the preaching of which the Holy Spirit operates to produce children, just as the apostle not only said: 'I begot you,' but also added: '...in Christ Jesus through the Gospel.' [1 Cor. 4:15] However, the thief Judas also preached the Gospel without harming the faithful."

Augustine also says, "On Baptism," *contra Donatistas*, Bk. 5, c. 20: "God gives the Holy Spirit even when a murderer, that is, one who hates his brother, performs a Baptism."

In his commentary on Psa. 10, he writes, saying: "Christ sent His betrayer, the same fellow whom He called 'a devil' and who could have revealed his faith before he handed over the Lord, and absent those words of Christ, along with the rest of the disciples to preach the kingdom of heaven. This He did that He might prove that the gifts of God do reach those who accept them with faith, even if they receive them through a preacher who is the sort of person such as Judas was."

And again he says: "If there is any merit of the giver and the receiver, let it be the merit of God the Giver and my conscience which receives, for these two—namely, His goodness and my faith—are not uncertain to me. Why are you introducing something about which I cannot be at all certain? Permit me to say: 'I trust in the Lord, etc.'"

Chrysostom also (homily 51, on Mat. 15) says: "Let us therefore touch the fringe of His garment—no, let us touch His entire being. If you want Him, He has presented not only His garment but His body to us, and not merely to touch but also to eat and be sated. Let us individual sick people come to Christ with great faith, for, if all those who touched the fringe of His robe then became fully well, how much the more strength shall we receive if we have the whole Christ within us?"

"Furthermore, to approach with faith is not that you receive His body in some way or other when it has been presented to you, but also much more, namely, that you touch Him with a pure heart; that you approach as if you should be coming to Christ Himself. For what if you don't hear His voice? You see Him lying there, don't you? In fact, you hear Him speaking through the very Evangelist. All of you, therefore, must believe that even now that Supper is being celebrated in which Christ Himself was sitting at table."

"Indeed, there is no difference at all between the former and this Supper, for the latter is being administered not by a man, but the former was administered by Him. When you see then the priest offering you the body [of Christ], do not think it is the hand of the priest but of Christ which is stretched out to you. For this is just as you received Baptism not from the priest, but it was God who held your head with His invisible power. This did not happen even at the hand of an angel for absolutely no one can do this. This is still true now."

"When a person is born again, this is the gift of God alone. You see, don't you, how those who adopt children into their family don't commit in any way this task to servants after this life but that they themselves are present to deal with all things at the judgment? Thus, God has committed this gift not to angels, but He Himself is present and orders and says: 'Do not call anyone "father" on earth,' not that you should despise your parents but that you should place Him who created and adopted you ahead of all others. After all, why will He who is the greatest, that is, who gave up His life for you, not disdain to hand over His body for you? Let us therefore listen to both priests and others as they tell us what a great and wonderful thing He has granted to us. Let us listen, please, and let us shudder greatly. He has surrendered to us His flesh, He has presented Himself as a sacrifice for us, etc."

So much for Chrysostom. In the meantime these statements have been about ministers of the Word and Sacraments.

Furthermore, those ancients also confessed that this is the external communion of the body and blood of Christ, that is, by which not only the worthy but also the unworthy eat the body and drink the blood of Christ.

Augustine speaks in this way against the Donatist Fulgentius: "Just as he who eats the body and drinks the blood of the Lord unworthily eats and drinks damnation to himself; so also, he who receives Baptism unworthily receives judgment and not salvation. Judas the Betrayer received the good body of Christ and Simon Magus received the good Baptism of Christ, but they were both destroyed not because they didn't use a good thing well, but because they were wicked men who used a good thing badly. Baptism is good, the body and blood of Christ are good, the Law is also good, but only if a person should use them most legitimately."

In his commentary on John, treatise 22, he says: "The apostle says to those who were handling the body poorly, something which the faithful knew, and because they were handling it badly: 'They were being chastised by the scourge of the Lord. For this reason many among you are weak, etc.'" He also says to Glorius, which is his Epistle 162: "Whoever were the saints of both Testaments who were not compelled to tolerate wicked people in their community? The Lord Himself tolerated Judas, who was a devil, a thief, and His betrayer. He permitted the innocent disciples to receive what the faithful knew was our ransom price."

He says, "on Baptism," *contra Donatistas*, Bk. 5, c. 8: "Just as Judas, to whom the Lord gave a morsel, gave the devil a place within himself not by accepting a bad thing but by accepting it badly; so each person who receives the Sacrament of the Lord unworthily does not cause it to be evil because he himself is evil nor cause himself to receive nothing because he did not receive it for his salvation. For they were nonetheless the body of the Lord and the blood of the Lord for those to whom the apostle was saying: 'He who eats unworthily eats and drinks damnation for himself.'"

Chrysostom, homily 83, on Mat. 26, speaks in this way to his priests that they may summon the wicked from Holy Communion: "If you yourself do not dare to keep him away; at least tell me: I shall not permit that to happen, I shall rather hand over my life before permitting anyone to receive the Lord's body unworthily. I would rather suffer my blood to be shed than grant that very sacred blood to anyone except the worthy person. If, on the other hand, someone should come ignorantly with his sins, it is not your fault, etc."

Now that I have spoken our way of thinking about the Lord's Supper with sufficiently many words and therefore often superfluous verbiage, had I not wished to head off as many false charges as I might, and after I have confirmed the same with the divine Word, I had it in mind to respond to some calumnies and disparagements of the Sacramentarians. Luther, however, has already offered that abundantly before this. The words of Christ's institution are very clear, but the father of darkness is trying to make them obscure. For as clear as are those words: "Take and eat; take and drink," so also are these clear: "This is My body; this is My blood."

Nevertheless, that I not appear to despise fully our adversaries in this area, I shall respond briefly for the sake of our brothers to some of those charges. After all, it is not our calling to respond to all the inappropriate calumnies of all our foes, not to mention their obvious blasphemous lies. Also, our brothers ought not do this, when they shall have seen that our way of thinking stands on, and remains with, the eternal Word of God.

First, they say that no more serious seduction has ever come upon people than that by which it has been said that Christ is in various places so that people now run to this and now to that altar and now from this church to that monastery because of that God-who-has-become-bread. It is in this way that they dare to blaspheme (as Satan is in the habit of doing) this institution of the supreme majesty of Christ. As they say, Christ foretold this seduction with these words of Mat. 24[:23–28]: "Then, if anyone will have said to you: 'Behold, here is Christ' or 'Behold, there He is,' don't believe him. For false Christs and false prophets will rise up and perform great miracles and wonders so that even the elect are led into error if that be possible. Behold, I have foretold this to you. If then they will have said to you: 'He is in the wilderness,' don't go out there; or: 'Behold, He is in the hidden places,' don't believe it. For, as lightning goes forth from the east and reaches all the way to the west, so also will be the coming of the Son of Man, for wherever the carcass is, there will the eagles also gather."

I respond that I have never heard nor read a greater blasphemy against Christ than this spewed from the mouth of the Sacramentarians against the institution of Christ, not even against ourselves, something which those blinded people think. Those great teachers are going to be driven back again to the whipping rods but, if you will have followed those blinded people, you will fall with them into the pit of despair and of all blasphemies. They will require here our moderation that they may be able to blaspheme more freely our Lord Jesus Christ. May I have no part with them, unless they should wish to repent!

Now let even some child come who may be able to understand human words, and I shall indicate to him that which no wisdom of any sort whatsoever will be able to deny, namely, that the Sacramentarians, who raise these objections to us against our Sacrament, are in this way making Christ one of the seducers, one of the false Christs, one of the false prophets. However, we must not on that account believe in this seducing Christ nor must we approach Him to believe His Word unless we should wish to be misled into error.

Indeed, from these words of Christ they make seducers all those who say that the bread of the Lord's Supper is the Lord's body and the cup His blood. However, Christ does say this. After taking the bread, He said: "This is My body," and, after taking the cup, He said: "This is My blood." If He were not to say this, there now would be no one to say it. According to them, therefore, Christ is a seducer and the head of all seducers who say and assert what He Himself says and asserts. This is as if Christ should wish to say: "Don't believe the misleaders who says: 'Behold here is Christ,' and: 'Behold there He is'; so that you don't even believe Me when I say: 'This is My body; this is My blood.' Behold, I have foretold this to you. Don't believe Me, because I am leading you into error."

I believe that Satan roared with laughter when he first persuaded the Sacramentarians to abuse this statement of Christ against this sacred institution of Christ. I believe he laughed, first, because he could move the minds of even some of the godly with that disguising of the truth against the institution of Christ if they should have respect for the abuse of the practitioners of the Mass, just as I knew certain people who did this. Next, I believe he laughed because he saw that this would be an outstanding blasphemy against Christ; and also because he could in this way persuade many that we were not correctly using this statement of Christ against those righteousness-peddling misleaders and false prophets who come in sheep's clothing but inwardly are ravening wolves, that they might in this way cause our Gospel to become suspect because we were finally accepting what Christ foretold, namely, that "Behold, He is here; He is there," was said against our Sacrament. Satan wanted this; and no one could give a handle to so great a blasphemy except Satan himself.

Be gone now, wicked rashness, and ruin your head with empty thoughts that you may make up something of Scriptures or of reasons which you may raise up to us against this sacred institution of Christ. You must find nothing else with your mad pursuit than pure blasphemies so that from the sole of your foot to the top of your head you will fill yourself inside and out with blasphemies. He who is filthy still is becoming more filthy. The Lord freely accepts those who stray and sin, but who will receive those who subvert His Word after receiving such an admonition?

Again I demand: give me some child. Isn't it he who says: "Look, here is Christ," and who says: "Look, there is Christ?" For this reason, they argue that he who says: "Look, here is Christ" is denying that Christ is over there; and the one who says: "Look, there is Christ" is denying that He is right here. Thus, when the one says: "Here is Christ," the other denies that and says: "Christ is not here but there"; and when the other says: "Christ is there," the other is denying that and saying: "Christ is not there but here."

But tell me now, when there ever has been such a dispute about our Sacrament among those who, because of the word and institution of Christ, have believed that the true body and blood of Christ are present? Some heretics have denied that consecration, as they call it; but among all those who were calling themselves "Catholics" and until now among the papists, although divided among sects, kept agreeing about the substance of the Sacrament.

The monks or Carthusians were not saying that they had the true body of Christ in the Sacrament but that others did not have it or that it was a better Sacrament at the highest altar than at the lowest. Certainly they were not 'seducers' by saying that according to the word of Christ the bread of the Supper is the body of Christ and the cup His blood, because to speak otherwise is to deny the word of Christ. However, they were seducers in this: that they took from us and prohibited to us the use of the cup when they said that he who may have wanted to follow the institution of Christ was a heretic. But now that the truth about this matter has been revealed, they surely must have seen that the axe has been set to the root of the tree.

Moreover, as we are correct in calling these people "seducers" who forbid the use of this Sacrament, so we much more correctly call "seducers" those who now have taken away with their denial the entire Sacrament which Christ instituted. Therefore they are falling into the pit which they dug for us.

If, then, someone of our brothers has been offended by this outcry of the Sacramentarians against us by which they cite against our Sacrament: "Look! He is here," and: "Look! He is there, etc.," let him turn his eyes away from those Mass-peddlers and Mass-purchasers, for in this way that quotation has an egregious appearance; and let him turn his eyes to the institution of Christ, and he will immediately see not only how rashly and falsely but also wickedly this was cited or objected, as we have now indicated. Our argument is now in favor of the institution and word of Christ, not in favor of the abuses of the Mass-minded. Furthermore, to say that the institution and word of Christ are a seduction is the blasphemy of Satan, something which the Sacramentarians are doing with this citation of theirs against us.

What, then, is the meaning of these words in Matthew? I respond. He is speaking about Christ and the kingdom of God, not about some Sacrament which Christ instituted. He is speaking about the preaching of the Antichrist (whom we must not believe), not about the words and institution of Christ (which is proper for all of us to believe). What Christ says here He calls "the kingdom of God" in Luke 17 [:20 ff.]. We read there: "The Pharisees asked Jesus when the kingdom of God would come. He responded: 'The kingdom of God will not come with observation, nor will people say: "Look! It is here"; or "Look! It is there"; for, behold, the kingdom of God is within you,' etc." As we read in Rom. 14[:17]: "The kingdom of God is righteousness and peace and joy in the Holy Spirit." This righteousness, peace, and joy is for us Christ, "whom God made for us righteousness, wisdom, sanctification, and redemption" (1 Cor. 1[:30]). "He is our peace" (Eph. 2[:14]); for, "justified by faith we have peace and joy through Christ" (Rom. 5[:1]).

God the Father established this kingdom of God or this King Christ within us. He sent Christ to us through the Word of the Gospel, and He now dwells within us. The pseudo-Christs (that is, the false Christians) and the false prophets (that is, the false preachers) have taken Him away from us. Among these last, the first were those pseudapostles, and then came all the righteousness-peddling teachers, especially those under the papists, who taught another righteousness other than Christ. That papist righteousness brought no certainty to afflicted consciences and, therefore, also no peace or joy. It cannot happen to the latter that they say the same things just as it happens to no sectarians; for it is necessary that those who have departed from the truthfulness in which unity lies not persist in their own wicked unity but be rent apart into many different directions.

Therefore, they will begin to teach: "Look! Here is Christ or the kingdom of God. Look! There it is." That is, they will begin to teach without the Word of God and contrary to it. One will teach in one way, and another will teach in another, about the righteousness of God, which truly is Christ; and they will teach whatever they may have dreamed. Meanwhile, because they teach nothing except human righteousness, therefore they cause the consciences of the hearers to become uncertain and doubting in different ways. You see, when those consciences are seeking the kingdom of God or Christ in one area, they have been misled into a different direction by the false Christs and false prophets. They finally begin to doubt and lose their way to find Christ, that is, what they should do as a result of which they please God, from what source they may recognize that their sins have been forgiven, and from whence to hope for their salvation.

They take up these works and those works—not those which God has commanded, but those which false teachers have prescribed without the Word of God. Through those teachers, their hearers learn to wash away their sins and to accumulate merit, as they say to themselves: "We are lifting up our fraternities, we are commanding Masses to be read, we are redeeming ourselves with pardons or indulgences, we are running to Rome, to St. James, and finally, when all those things provide no answer, we run into a monastery and then into the Carthusian ranks, because we do not think that Christ or the kingdom of God is outside those ideas."

But that kingdom is something which comes without observation, whether you observe from the right, that is, from the pomp of the world, or from the left, that is, flee the world just as some have already fled the world but have taken the world with them in their heart, judging that they in this way are better than the others whom they have left behind and whom they ought to have served. Why have the individual orders of monks until now been shouting against others, or why have they become divided against each other, and who doesn't know what some are saying against others?

Nevertheless, these human righteousnesses and false opinions about Christ have been confirmed through great signs and lying wonders, as we read in 2 The. 2[:9].

Christ or the kingdom of God is not in the wilderness, that you may escape thereto outside the world, nor is it in the secret places that you may set yourself apart from the world, but wherever He rules. Now that He has received power in heaven and on earth, He is bound to no place and to no observations. You will certainly find Him there where He reveals Himself through His Word. Where it happens that you believe in Him, that you serve your neighbor, that you suffer for the truth—there is Christ or the kingdom of God.

This Christ and this kingdom of God are now being despised when compared with the superstition of human righteousness and the parade of human ceremonies. However, those who may have adhered through faith in His Word to the invisible and omnipresent Christ and the kingdom of God which is not glorious in the sight of the world will, at the end of the age, cling to the visible and appearing kingdom in the glory of the Father, caught up as they will have been to meet Christ in the air. In this way, they will always be eagles with the Lord, and that is our comfort.

Therefore, this one passage which the Sacramentarians have produced against us (so to speak) makes clear what egregious blasphemers they are and that they don't know anything about what they are affirming. Thus, until you stop making Christ one of the misleaders, you will not show from this passage of Matthew that the bread of the Supper is not the Lord's body, nor the cup His blood. After all, it has not been a false christ nor a false prophet who has said this to us, but that true Christ, the true Prophet whom God has raised up, our one Teacher and Schoolmaster about whom the Father says: "Listen to Him"; I say, it is He who says: "This is My body; this is My blood." This is not misleading but the word of life and salvation, provided you believe.

Afterwards they attack us in this way: Mark [14:23] speaks in this way about the cup: "He took the cup and, when He had given

thanks, He gave it to them, and they all drank of it. And He said
to them: 'This is My blood of the new testament, which is shed
for many.'" They say: "If you are asserting that blood is in the cup
by virtue of the words of Christ, what had the disciples drunk before Christ said: 'This is My blood?' Therefore, it seems from that
passage of Mark that, after they had eaten, the Lord said: 'This is
My body'; and, after they had drunk: 'This is My blood.' Therefore
they did not eat the body of Christ nor did they drink His blood.
Therefore, these words have an interpretation different from that
the bread is the body of Christ, and the cup His blood." However,
if you should ask: "What other interpretation?," you will hear truly
madmen, some saying one thing, others saying something else.

Therefore, I respond: With what conscience do they say these
things from Mark? Who will make them certain about this way of
thinking? They are adding to the Word of God so that they corrupt
it. Tell me, please, what sin did the good evangelist Mark commit
in these words? After all, they are trying to make him hateful to
the Church of Christ, as if he said something contrary to Matthew,
Luke, Paul, and even against himself and, in so doing, something
contrary to this sacred institution of Christ. It is not strange that
they are ruining the reputations of good men and making them
suspect today, if they have the same opinion as those when they attempt the same thing against Mark, the writer of a sacred Gospel.

That's the way things are with regard to that passage of
Mark. What the others have said, this Mark also says here, for he
tells that the Lord said about the cup: "This is My blood, etc." The
others have also told this. Although he first tells that they drank,
but later tells that the Lord said: "This is My blood, etc."; nevertheless, he does not say that, after they drank, the Lord said to them:
"This is My blood," but said simply: "And He said to them: 'This is
My blood, etc.'" Now, why are you opposing Mark to the rest when
he clearly says the same as the rest, namely, that the Lord said: "This

is My blood, etc."? You have nothing different from Mark. He says: "And He said to them…" Who denies that the Lord said this? We embrace it with all our heart.

Furthermore, if you wish to know whether the Lord said this before or after they drank, you will not see this in Mark. He does not say: "And the Lord said after they had drunk," nor: "The Lord said before they had drunk"; but only this: "And the Lord said to them…" Therefore, all four of those[8] bear witness that the Lord said this about the cup. However, Mark does not say in what order the Lord spoke, that is, before they drank; but the other three say it with clear words so that no one except an outstandingly stupid person would have denied it.

Matthew speaks in this way: "After He took the cup, He gave thanks and gave it to them *saying* (Blind man, do you see the connection?): "Drink of this, all of you, for this is My blood, etc." Luke also speaks in this way: "In like manner, He took the cup after they had eaten and said: 'This cup is the new testament in My blood, which is shed for you.'" Paul, too, speaks in this way: "When the supper was finished, He took the cup in like manner and said: 'This cup is the new testament in My blood.'"

Therefore those obfuscators are interpreting clear words with obscure ones. Whoever may have accepted their interpretation will have made liars out of Matthew, Luke, and Paul. They also make St. Mark the contradicting author of this wickedness. For Mark himself tells about the bread: "Take. Eat. This is My body," so that you see that he did not want that which they are dreaming to themselves on the basis of his words.

They appear to have become children twice, for they are unwilling to see what is most common in all writers of history, namely, that they often narrate later activities before prior ones, and yet they are not lying, provided that the things they tell did happen

8 That is, Matthew, Mark, Luke, and Paul.

but do not say in what order it happened; or, if they do say, they meanwhile indicate that they are writing what they omitted earlier.

Were I to say: "On Sunday we have dinner in the evening, lunch at noon, and fast in the morning when we listen to the sacred discourse," what sin would I commit with that narrative? In the meantime, you—you foolish debater—because of that narrative of mine, which is true, claim that the order of the activities has been turned around and thus the very nature of things, and say: "Evening therefore, is before noon, and noon is before the morning hours. And we have dinner and lunch first; and do you hear that we fast at the sacred services after dinner and lunch?"

Similarly, if I were to tell the truth that Christ was crucified and that Christ was born of a virgin, would you infer from that true narrative that it is false that Christ therefore was first born of a virgin and was crucified later? That is clearly what is happening from the true narrative of Mark: "They all drank of it, and Christ said to them, etc." Therefore we infer that, after they had drunk, He said to them.

What Mark says is true: "They all drank of it"; and what he says is true: "And He said to them: 'This is My blood.'" No one should deny that they all drank; and no one should deny that Christ said: "This is My blood." Matthew, Luke, and Paul convince us that it is a lie that Christ spoke these words after they had drunk, but that Mark does not say this is your lie. Therefore those are unwilling to see in this passage of Mark that inverted order which the Greeks call "πρωθύσερομ," even if such great lamps be placed before their eyes.

Therefore, they have nothing from Mark with which to defend themselves. In fact, with these trifling remarks of theirs, they make clear with what anxiety they struggle to establish their lies against the truthfulness of God.

If this were not enough, I hear them saying: "Why don't you hand yourselves over to Satan and call yourselves wicked? If any of the things which you teach were true, namely, that the bread is the body of Christ and the cup His blood, and that we are so weak that we cannot yet grasp them; would you not lift up the weak?" I hear those things, but there is a different reckoning with regard to the straying, the sinners, and the weak. We are dealing against fighters and the like as they want to appear to be winners and defenders of their own wickedness. If they are weak, they are not the schoolmasters of the world, and they do not stop upsetting good consciences in the one people but are doing that everywhere with their public writings, their wicked teaching, and their denial of the truthfulness of Christ.

May they check their tongues which stir up blasphemies, and may they give glory to the word of Christ! If they will not stop, we shall sing to them the judgment of God in the name of the Lord from the words of Paul, who says: "Moreover, he who upsets you, will bear his judgment, whoever he might be." [Gal. 5:10]

Finally, angry as they are at the institution of Christ, they burst forth and say: "What benefit do we gain that in the Supper we eat the body of Christ and drink His blood when that remembrance of Christ can happen with bread and wine?" What am I hearing? Perhaps that can happen even with wood and stone. Why wouldn't that happen in the presence of the body and blood of Christ? They say: "Because remembrance is of absent things." Who told you that? But, let it be! Good Sacramentarians that you are, don't you know that there must be here a remembrance or announcement of the death of Christ? The death of Christ as it happened once on the cross is not present now, although we celebrate the mystery according to this institution of Christ. After all, Christ is not dying anymore. Death no longer has dominion over Him. If a commemoration is for absent things, as you say; we are commemorating the death of Christ.

But what shall we respond to those who are asking: "For what reason are the body and blood of Christ in the Supper?" First, find fault with Christ, who instituted His Supper in this way and dignified His Church with this honor. Moreover, He also wanted the Supper in this way to be a stone of offense and a rock of scandal for the wicked.

Next, He wanted His body and blood to be there that we not despise this Sacrament and also that you—or at least your people—not despise it, something which Paul says in this way after he had narrated Christ's institution (because I have told that Christ said: "This is My body; this is My blood"): "Whoever will have eaten the bread," not just any bread but *this* bread, and "whoever drinks the cup," not any cup but *the cup of the Lord*, "unworthily, will be guilty of the body and blood of the Lord," not only of the bread and cup alone, for Christ said about that bread: "This is My body," and about that cup: "This or here is My blood." But if those who take it unworthily receive judgment upon themselves, what else will those who commune worthily here receive except eternal life?

Furthermore, Christ instituted here a commemoration of Himself—something which no one denies. Will you have said that this is nothing? No. Therefore, the body and blood of Christ are not here because a remembrance was instituted, and that is for absent things, as they say. Here we are not celebrating the memory or rather the remembrance of the body and blood of Christ simply, which Satan can also remember and say, but the memory of the body of Christ which was handed over on the cross for us as well as the blood of Christ which was shed on the cross for us. That is, we are celebrating the commemoration or announcement of the death of Christ.

For this commemoration, therefore, He not only instituted His body and blood but also commanded and handed over His body and blood for us to eat and drink invisibly and under the Sacrament but also to do that truly, lest we have any doubt about those things which He handed over in that Supper for us to eat and drink in remembrance, because He handed them over on the cross for us. I cannot state enough here the usefulness of this Sacrament if you should use it correctly.

When Christ says: "Take, eat, drink," Sacramentarian wickedness says: "I am indeed eating and drinking not for myself but for my brothers, because the Sacraments of Christ are nothing but signs among those people by which we know that we are Christians." This is not true, if in the meantime you deny them and that there is a covenant between God and people, something which the Sacraments truly are if you truly accept them, just as the gifts of the bridegroom are the very sure signs of his love not so much for others as for his bride, for which reason the bride believes that love is hers to the extent that that can be. After all, with reference to circumcision, it is not unknown that in Scripture it is a covenant between God and man, namely, a sign of shame which is revealed in the behavior of men, especially among virgins, if God instituted it for this alone: that it be a sign among men by which one is known to be a Jew.

I am not denying that the usefulness of covenants and signs extends also to others, but I am telling between whom they are covenants and signs, namely, between God who gives or institutes them, and the person who receives them.

Therefore, in this institution of this Sacrament, Christ is instituting two things: the one, that you eat His body and drink His blood; and the other is that remembrance that you announce the death of the Lord. From these there comes a twofold usefulness and this very great indeed, the one for you and the other for others.

Your benefit is not that of others, because you are eating His body and drinking His blood, for you are receiving the covenant of Christ and the absolutely certain sign of salvation, for you are sure that Christ (whose body and blood you receive according to His institution) is yours. God also wanted to deal with us through such external covenants and signs through His Word that we may also believe that our bodies (which are the temple of the Holy Spirit and which are also baptized as are our souls into Christ) belong to the resurrection. "For we are the members of His body, of His flesh and of His bones" (Eph. 5[:30]). The Word has been made flesh that He might save the whole person for Himself.

Are you willing to hear that from this institution? Christ says: "It is broken for you. It is shed for you for the remission of sins." He is saying: "These are for you who will eat and drink according to My institution and command." If you cause some lack of clarity in these words of Christ; hear Paul, the interpreter, as he says: "He who receives unworthily eats and drinks damnation for himself, not for others; for I am not defiled if others come with me unworthily to this communion." If, however, this word of Paul is true, it follows that the person who comes worthily eats and drinks eternal life for himself and not for others, just as Peter used to eat and drink eternal life for himself, but not Judas, the betrayer. Therefore you eat and drink for yourself, not for others, whether you do that well or poorly.

The utility of others does not lie in the fact that you eat and drink but in the commemoration by which you announce the Lord's death that others may also believe or, if they believe, they may be strengthened. In this way, when the death of the Lord has been made clear among us, namely, that He shed His blood for us for the forgiveness of our sins, we are not easily misled by pseudapostolic preaching which foists upon us human satisfactions and invented righteousnesses without the Word of God and therefore contrary thereto instead of the righteousness of God, which is Christ Jesus, whom the Father handed over into death for us that we may be free from sin, death, and hell, and that we may become children of God. You see, the whole Gospel has perished after the true use of this Sacrament has been wickedly abolished and forbidden to us in our churches.

From these points, we now also may see that those who ridicule us when we say that the signs of God strengthen us are accomplishing nothing. They also say that Paul is saying that we are strengthened and sealed through the Holy Spirit. However, if they had sensed even a tiny bit what that strengthening and sealing of the Holy Spirit is (despite the fact that they wish to appear very Spirit-filled), they would rejoice about our way of thinking, and they would not laugh wickedly and think that their thoughts were the Holy Spirit, as they despised the Word of God without which we magnify no signs.

After all, who denies that the Holy Spirit strengthens and seals us? For this strengthening, however, the Spirit uses the Word of God as it is preached or written and the signs of God with which He assures, strengthens, comforts, and seals wavering consciences. Otherwise, if you receive the Spirit without the Word of God, or if you say that you have been strengthened and sealed without the Word of God, consider of what spirit you may be. The Word of God, as also a sign added to the Word, is not effective for me without the Spirit of God, for I do not believe without the Spirit.

But, again, the Spirit of God wants to accomplish nothing in me for my salvation without the Word of God. The Spirit of God is omnipotent, to be sure. He cannot act otherwise. However, because of my rashness, He will not change the order which He has promised us and which Paul depicts on these levels, Rom. 10[:14–15a]: "How will they call upon Him in whom they have not believed? And how will they believe in Him about whom they have not heard? And how will they hear without a preacher? And how will they preach unless they will have been sent?"

Why, then, are they accusing us of asserting here the strengthening of consciences? The way the Spirit elsewhere comforts and strengthens us with the Word He does here with the Word and sign. This deigning of Christ, who surrenders to us His body and blood, and our remembrance about Christ among ourselves certainly are a great consolation and confirmation in every temptation.

Here, because of the word of Christ, these things are truly present which we remember He once gave up on the cross, just as you become mindful of a friend at his presence and recall with thanksgiving what kindnesses he once showed you.

Go now and tell for what reason the body and blood of the Lord are in the Supper. Is it that you may become a disputer and misleader of minds? When you cannot understand the kindness of Christ toward us, do you go on to *accuse* Him whom you ought to be *thanking?*

These things which I have written are my testimony to the whole world that, when the Sacramentarians deny that the bread is the body of Christ in the Lord's Supper and the cup His blood, and that we receive these things for eternal life if we receive them just as Christ instituted that Supper; —I say, this is my witness that I do not have the same way of thinking with those who deny this. After this, let no one bother me with the idea that I am going in a different direction. I believe the word of Christ, from which I would depart for the dreams of men only wickedly. I now rejoice to have published this testimony of my faith. To those who reproach me, I shall after this respond steadfastly with the word of Christ.

May God illumine the hearts of all with His truthfulness, and may He strengthen us in every good work through Jesus Christ, our Lord! Amen.

NOW FOLLOW A FEW WORDS OF JOHANNES BUGENHAGEN OF POMERANIA ABOUT SOME INDIVIDUAL SACRAMENTARIANS
ALONG WITH AN EXPLANATION OF THE SIXTH CHAPTER OF JOHN THE EVANGELIST

Now, finally, my fine reader, I am revealing to you what I promised before, that is, a new kind of Sacramentarian. They
promise that they wish to accept all the words of the sacred institution of Christ in their appropriate and natural meaning so that we
may yield to them, and yet that they may deny, as do the others, that
the bread of the Lord is His body and the cup His blood.

These say that Christians and believing Christians—in fact,
correctly-believing Christians—eat there the true body of Christ and
drink the true blood of Christ in the living Word of God through
true faith. In the meantime, however, they are playing games with these
words as if they are responding to the institution of Christ but nevertheless wanting nothing other than that the bread of the Lord which
we eat is not the body of Christ and the cup of the Lord which we
drink is not the blood of Christ, and this against the clear words of the
institution of Christ. Lest the common folk sense that this is a denial
of the word of Christ (and, therefore, of Christ Himself), they disguise it by speaking German words, but the Hebrew and German
wording are the same:"…*im lebendigen Wort Gottes durch einen wahren
Glauben* — …in the living Word of God through a true faith."

In the meantime, however, they are denying the Word of God. However, if they deny the Word, tell me, please, what faith do they have? They are acting if we are asserting something in this case without the Word of God, or as if we are teaching that we must use so great a Sacrament without faith, something some of them have been asserting about us recently in their public writings, but that is a truly shameless lie. This they did after the whole world agreed that Martin Luther is not teaching this. Certainly Zwingli ought not to have lied against conscience after he had read the book which Luther wrote against Carlstadt, as he himself confesses in a published writing.

I said this above, and now I am repeating it briefly. If, in the body or congregation of our Church which does not deceive us, we teach, believe, and confess that the bread of the Lord is the body of the Lord and that the cup of the Lord is the blood of the Lord, that is indubitably so, because we believe what He Himself says, and we do that which He Himself commands. The Sacramentarians do neither, for they do not believe that the bread is the body of Christ (something which Christ says), nor do they believe that they are eating the body of Christ (something which Christ commands), because He did not say: "Eat the bread," but: "Eat My body."

Moreover, that you here do not eat the body and drink the blood of the Lord unworthily, you are required not only to have faith that you believe that this is true, but that you also have that faith as a result of which we are the children of God and which we call "justifying faith," and that is trust in the blood of Jesus Christ. You may be able to say "incipient faith," which in the meantime is not life-giving nor justifying, but when that incipient faith has been perfected, it undoubtedly includes justifying faith, just as you read in Heb. 11[:6]: "Without faith it is impossible to please God." You see, it is necessary that one who is approaching God believe that God exists and that He is the Rewarder of those who seek Him.

We teach with this assurance which Christ teaches in John 6, that repentant sinners must approach the Sacrament of bread and wine which He Himself instituted at the Last Supper that He might declare with a sure and visible sign that He still deals with us in our weakness. When I say "sign," I do not deny the truth which only faith sees present there on the basis of Christ's institution. This I say lest the lies of calumniators attack me.

However, if you say: "As Christ teaches in John 6, it is with this assurance that the faithful always eat and drink the flesh and blood of the Lord, for they believe or have faith in the flesh and blood of Christ," then you are speaking accurately and in a Christian way. However, if you add: "It therefore is unnecessary at some time to eat His body and drink His blood in the Sacrament of bread and wine"; then let Christ respond to you: "He who instituted it in this way surely wanted to advise Me in this way."

With that disguise of theirs, namely, "in the living Word of God through true faith," those who deny the word of Christ ought not deny to us the living Word of God: "This is My body, etc.," lest they have no faith at all.

Why, however, shall I not produce now those who are of the people about whom I am saying these things especially? You see, all the Sacramentarians rarely respond to the subject which they themselves have undertaken to prove; namely, that the bread of the Lord is not the body of the Lord. In the meantime, they say much about words of faith and some things about which there is no disagreement that in the meantime they may disguise other things as if writing much in favor of their cause. Nevertheless, there are some who with great enthusiasm leave far behind them all the rest of the Sacramentarians, for they do not accept that "This" stands for "body," and that "is" stands for "signifies"; nor that "body" stands for "the signified body" nor "this" for "that," as my dear friend Conrad von Offenbach, whom I see they called by a different name later, if the same intent and foolishness of both names should deceive me. Although he is completely inept and ignorant of all things, nevertheless he thinks that he is worthy of receiving a response from someone for his inabilities, as if the world does not see his insanity even if no one should admonish it.

Those individual Sacramentarians whom I now indicate you should avoid (nevertheless without naming them, for I prefer them to be my brothers rather than adversaries) speak in this way. They say: "As far as we are concerned, these words of Christ: 'This is My body' retain their natural meaning just as the Lord uttered them, as did also the evangelists and Paul, who wrote from the Holy Spirit. We accept them very simply without any addition. We compare these words of Christ with similar words of Christ which are written in John 6: 'My flesh truly is food, and My blood truly is drink,' because in the Supper there cannot be a body and blood different from those about which John had spoken earlier in his Gospel."

"We divide the Lord's Supper into a spiritual eating and drinking, and into a worthy remembrance without the breaking of bread and the drinking of the cup of the Lord, as Paul calls it. According to the eating, we know, believe, and confess that truly believing Christians eat the true body of Christ and drink His true blood in the living word of God through true faith. From this, it is made most certainly clear to the faithful who that food and Supper are, for it is necessary to know well that food which satisfies the faithful to eternal life."

"Christians do in commemoration that which Christ did and later commanded them to do in remembrance of Him after He gave His body and shed His blood for the forgiveness of sins, just as the Lord and Paul have expressed these more broadly and clearly in their words. Christ instituted the Supper in this way, Paul arranged it for the Corinthians, the holy fathers in the very early church observed it; and Tertullian, Cyprian, Hilary, Augustine and more wrote about it."

You have it all. They did not publish more ideas recently. All the rest were nothing else but words, although we nevertheless had hoped for more because of the abundance of such great enthusiasm. Moreover, I would prefer them to have published under their own name, for we are not unaware how authors do publish under a different name and furthermore, under the name of "pastors." Why are those who themselves are at fault stirring up unpopularity for other good men? But it now seemed convenient for them that they preserve that propriety by which to advise themselves but not others.

I am not unaware of what they are teaching about the Holy Eucharist, nor are they unaware that I know this; for in their letters and whole treatises which they have sent around privately they are in the habit of discussing at very great length their cause among those whom they are trying to draw to themselves. I was one of those whom they tempted in this way.

I do not believe that they will accuse me of treachery as if I am revealing the secrets of friends because they themselves are teaching this in public and especially because they wish to appear to be preaching the truth and glory of God, but that I am in error. Therefore, they will rejoice because I am writing briefly of their glory and my disgrace.

They themselves indeed agree with the other Sacramentarians and deny that the bread of the Lord is the body of Christ. They therefore consider them as good associates of the bread and wine, but they take away from them the authority of the Spirit and arrogate it for themselves. One of their standard-bearers addressed this point in this way: "Zwingli says that a good man does not boast about some revelation but writes in this way: 'I tell you a dream, etc.' We, on the other hand, do have the spirit of revelation."

This revelation addressing the point had also been written in this way: "Inasmuch as one was excessively concerned about his case for the Eucharist, as it were; it seemed best to him, as if the

Holy Spirit were admonishing him, that he read, and he immediately opened a book of the blessed martyr Cyprian. There he found in Bk. 1, epistle 6, a source from which he could be certain later that the bread of the Lord is not His body." You see the certainty of this spirit whom he is not permitted to doubt now, even if Christ may say something different. Read all of Cyprian. I should despair if in this case he does not speak what we speak. On the basis of the words of Cyprian, what was that spirit of revelation?

In fact, let us speak about their words which we set forth above. If the ideas which they propose are true, why don't we get crowns ready for them? Why don't we decree a triumphal march for them? The discord has been resolved. We have not so much as a word because of which to murmur against the Sacramentarians. Indeed, the Sacramentarians will be sorry that they have lost their glory which some have sought through "safely," others through "signifies," and still others through other arguments. They will become ashamed that up to this point they are corrupters of the sacred institution of Christ because of their human dreams when they now hear from them that we must accept the words of Christ without any figures of speech. However, they will grieve less when they see, no matter how poorly the battle has gone, that victory stares them in the face and that we are succumbing—we against whom they have battled more seriously than against the papists, because Satan has attended us with a greater hatred.

"Lutherans" (as they are called, whether or not they wish), will be compelled to yield and surrender. In this they have been quite unfortunate, although their power and weapons have been unharmed; but they cannot boast of victory. They have fought well with excellent arguments. They have required only that people accept the words of Christ's institution very simply, they approve of weapons and battling, and victory yields to those who have fought poorly, as the spirit of revelation witnesses which had said to its priest: "What if neither Zwingli nor Luther should agree rightly about the Eucharist?"

The words now remain unharmed for us in their natural meaning. "This," that is, this bread, signifies "bread." "Is" is taken substantively. "My body" is taken for the true body of Christ, not as His signified body. What else do we require? And yet the bread is not the body of Christ, something which we undertook to defend from the words of Christ taken in their natural sense. This is not another excuse for us not to become Sacramentarians. Tell me, please, to whom do both we and the Sacramentarians owe that victory and peace except to those upon whom so great a spirit has breathed? What is so strange if the whole world should marvel that, after such great disagreements, all things have come together into one harmony through these so suddenly?

Although I may still be so stubborn that I am not yielding; yet, lest I appear to be totally thankless for so great a revelation, I give thanks in the name of all Lutherans and therefore of all Christians, first, that they teach that people must accept these words: "This is My body" in their natural meanings just as the Lord uttered them and as the Holy Spirit inspired the evangelists and Paul to speak very simply, because in this way they condemn all other Sacramentarians, as many as have been writing until now. Next, I give thanks that they confess in clear language that in the Supper there cannot be a different body and blood from those about which the Lord spoke earlier in John, for here we are permitted to go no farther. In John, however, the Lord spoke about His true flesh and blood. In the Supper, therefore, the true body and blood of Christ are present when the Lord says: "This is My body; this cup is My blood." By this reasoning, you spiritualists wait in vain for other Sacramentarians to thank you when you immediately surrender to us both your weapons and your entire cause in this way. Yet, in the meantime, you fight against us because of your pleasant dream.

Moreover, you would behave against us in this way on the basis of John 6 if the Lord there were to hand over, as He does in the Supper, the bread and wine, and if it were agreed from the certain words of Christ that these two statements were true: first, that the bread and wine in John 6 were the same bread and wine which are in the Supper; and second, that the bread and wine in John 6 were not the body and blood of Christ. Then you certainly might infer that the bread and wine of John 6 are not the body and blood of Christ, and therefore, the wine and bread in the Supper are not the body and blood of Christ. But now, because you have nothing of this in John 6, why, on the basis of John 6, are you trying to prove against us that the bread which we break, that is, about which Christ says: "This is My body" is not the body of Christ, and that the cup which we bless, about which Christ says: "This cup is My blood" is not the blood of Christ? When, I ask, does Christ deny in John 6 what He asserts in the Supper? —not to mention that this cannot be.

Therefore we thank you for asserting that we must take the words of Christ very simply here without any figure and that in the Supper there cannot be a body and blood different from those about which the Lord spoke in John. In the meantime, it troubles you that in the Supper, but not in John 6, the Lord presents bread and institutes an external Sacrament about which bread He clearly wants us to believe what we do not see externally and which the senses do not grasp but which faith alone grasps, namely, that it is His body because of the words: "This is My body." Meanwhile, argue with Him who wanted it to be that way. We certainly are giving an account of our faith on the basis of the word of Christ. If this doesn't please you, go somewhere else.

Now I also want to offer the reason for my stubbornness as to why I cannot and must not yield to these words spoken so well on our behalf (as I have said), and yet which do not agree with us. They say: "We are comparing these words of Christ with other words of Christ which are written in John 6: 'My flesh is truly flesh, and My blood is truly drink.'" In the meantime, they say nothing as to how they are comparing them.

They compare them just as they are in the habit of writing and teaching. They say: "'Is' cannot be taken as 'signifies,' nor 'body' as 'the signified body.' Rather, we must take all the words in their natural meaning." As we have said, these things please us. However, they go on: "Thus, from John 6 we shall take the genuine sense of the words of the Supper. There Christ says: 'My flesh is truly food, and My blood is truly drink.' He does not say: 'The food is My flesh,' nor 'the bread is My body and the drink My blood.' In the Supper, therefore, it is the same, although the words may have been expressed in this order: 'This' or 'this bread is My body. This cup is My blood.' Nevertheless, as far as the understanding and sense of the words are concerned, we must construe them in this way: 'My body is this,' that is, 'bread,' just as He says in John 6: 'My flesh is food.' Also: 'The new testament in My blood which is shed for you for the remission of sins is this cup,' so that the meaning briefly is this: 'My blood is the cup,' just as he says in John 6: 'My blood truly is drink.'"

In the meantime, here we wonder where they may be leading us away. They do not stop there, and they charge falsely that there is great danger to our salvation because we do not permit simple bread to be in the Lord's Supper because of the word which says: "This is My body" and because we do not permit simple wine to be there because of the word which says: "This cup is My blood." They themselves are making for us out of the true body of Christ a physical and visible bread which all people eat everyday, and out of the true blood of Christ shed for sins they make for us a physical and common drink which all people drink every day. Thus the body of the Son of God is common bread, and the blood of the Son of God (and thus of God, as Paul says in Acts 20) is common drink.

What else will you see from this interpretation, if, as they say, the words must remain in their proper and natural meaning? "This" undoubtedly indicates "bread," so that it most certainly signifies "this"; that is, "this bread." But they don't permit this bread to be anything other than bread, however great the reverence they attach to the Lord's Sacrament, as they say, obviously because they have been compelled to do this by other words of Paul.

Therefore, "My body is this bread" does not have another sense according to the natural meaning of the words than this: "My body is external bread," unless this bread which Christ breaks is not external bread. This would be still more obvious in the handing over of the cup, where He says not only "this," as in the handing over of the bread, but also adds "cup," so that according to them He is saying: "My blood is this cup." If this cup is not external, they do not say: "The blood of Christ is the external cup." We are certain that they do not allow bread other than external bread and any other cup but an external cup in the Supper, however much we may cry out against this on the basis of the words of Christ.

Do you see finally where they are casting out from us the body and blood of Christ? Here I would dispute with them as to what profit there is in eating a body made of bread and in drinking a blood made of wine, but this is not yet the end of the story. You see, they don't want that which I have said, but no one can conclude from that inversion of theirs anything other than what I have said, because at the same time they are boasting that they are taking all the words in the primary sense.

They therefore speak in this way: "We are not teaching that one must read: 'My body is this bread,' but just as the words have it: 'My body is this'; and, although we read about the cup, 'This cup' and not simply 'this,' nevertheless we claim that we must place a comma after 'this' and before 'cup,' that is, between 'this' and 'cup,' so that it reads [in Greek]: 'τουτο, τὸ ποτηριον' so that you read and understand: 'The new testament in My blood which is shed for you for the remission of sins is this.' What? Namely, 'the cup.'" Here it would have been very convenient to have omitted 'cup.'

Next, they say: "When we teach that we must construe: 'My body is this,' we do not take this to mean 'this,' that is 'this bread,' but simply 'this,' that is, 'bread.' And we do not take it to mean physical but spiritual bread which feeds one's spirit, so that, when Christ distributes the bread He says: 'My body is this,' that is, 'bread,' namely, 'spiritual bread.' Thus, this fits well with that which He says in John 6: 'My flesh truly is food.' So also we understand the words of Christ about the cup in this way: 'The new testament in My blood which is shed for you is this,' namely, 'the cup.' Obviously this is not the cup which Christ is holding or giving but a spiritual cup, just as Christ says in John 6: 'My blood is truly drink.'"

Now, my fine reader, I have placed before your eyes sufficiently bluntly how they are comparing the words of the Lord's Supper with John 6. As far as they are concerned, this statement is not true: "The bread is the body of Christ, even if Christ be saying: 'This bread is My body,' just as He says later: 'This cup…' or: 'This chalice, etc.'" I say, this is not true unless you turn it around and read it all backwards in this way: "The body of Christ is bread, etc.," but in such a way that the words do not signify bread and cup which Christ distributes in the Supper, but other things; namely, spiritual bread and spiritual cup.

I am not saying now how these statements fit together in the institution of Christ: "Take. Eat. My body is spiritual bread. Take. Drink. My blood is spiritual blood," unless you should add many things on the basis of your own thinking, just as they are in the habit of doing. Of course, you may think they fit together if someone should say, as he hands you common bread: "Take and eat. A fly is buzzing about"; and later adds in confirmation of his words: "One goes into the ancient forest where there are deep dens of wild beasts"; and: "Who is so ignorant that he doesn't know that for grammarians there are eight parts of speech?" In the meantime, all these statements are true, namely, that a fly buzzes around, that people go into an ancient forest, etc. But you—unless you are clearly stupid—will require those statements to fit together with each other, for you may not infer anything nor prove anything from anything at all. Therefore we don't require of them whether the things which they are saying about spiritual food and drink are true, and that the elements of this world cannot justify; in fact, that only the carnal eating of the Sacrament is not the forgiveness of sins, etc. We know and teach that these things are true without the Sacramentarians.

Although I often wonder to myself that some people boast of their lies against us with such shamelessness, I should also wonder that, because of those things which we are asserting about our Sacraments, they are lying that we trust in the elements of this world and hope for righteousness in the little bit of water of Baptism and in the bread and wine, but as if we consider those external things without the word, institution, and command of Christ our Lord. We trust in this Word which is not an element of this world, but is the truth of God which endures forever. Otherwise, absent that Word, we would permit the bread to be bread for ourselves just as a stone is a stone, a fig is a fig, etc. Your opinions, however, are much clearer to you than is the word of Christ.

What, then, are we requiring of them? Only that they certify their own consciences first, and then the consciences of others who agree with those things which they say about those words with which Christ instituted for us this sacred banquet; next, whether the changing of words corresponds to that order of words with which the evangelists write that Christ expressed; and finally, that they tell us when they are going to provide what they have promised; namely, that they are willing to take all the words of the institution of this Sacrament very simply in their proper and natural meanings so that they add nothing, etc. After all, I see that with that promise they have indeed condemned all the other Sacramentarians that they alone may have the glory which others have sought so eagerly but for which they have mocked us with a false hope. From the very beginning of that discourse, they make out of the bread which is broken for us a spiritual bread. Is this clearly taking all the words of Christ in the natural sense?

However, I argue with them in this way: if, as you say, according to the natural meaning, because of the institution of Christ, the bread for you is spiritual bread, on what does your spirit feed? After all, you say: "My body is this," that is, bread, and that no one take this to mean external bread, you add "spiritual"; but, at the same time, you say that the words remain in their own natural meaning. If the natural meaning is this, namely, that the bread which is broken signifies not external bread but spiritual so that this bread to you is spiritual bread, how do you prove here that Christ declares with these words: "This is My body," that He is saying: "My body is spiritual bread?"

Otherwise, I do not see how the bread which Christ is holding in His hands does not rather signify in its natural meaning material bread rather than spiritual bread; —I say, if those words are true just as you promised; namely, that you wished to take them all very simply. If the bread in the Supper is spiritual bread, how will that stand firm which you are explaining: "My body is this," that is, spiritual bread, when there is no doubt that "this" signifies this bread which we handle with our mouth and hands? Tell me, please, why are you accusing us of confessing that the bread of the Lord in the Supper is the body of Christ when we are depending not on our own dreams but on the sure words of Christ?

What is spiritual bread except Christ, just as you are saying from John 6: "My flesh truly is food, etc."? If, then, the bread of the Supper is spiritual bread for you, why is it not the body of Christ for us? If your inverted word orders and additions should have such great weight, why would not that very simple institution of Christ (which we say it is wrong to violate with some corrupted words) have value for us?

[They reply:] "But, are you not listening, our Pomeranian friend? We are not saying that the body of Christ is this bread which we are handling in the Supper, so that you take 'My body is this' to mean 'this bread,' but is bread, so that you take it to mean here bread, but not corporal but spiritual bread." I hear you, and I understand; but in this way you are not keeping the natural meaning of the words, for the natural meaning of the word "this" in the words of the Lord (something which no one should deny) signifies not just any bread but only this bread which is distributed in the Supper.

Therefore, permit us to take the words in that order in which Christ expressed them and the evangelists wrote them, and let us show you what you yourselves cannot show, namely, that we take the words of Christ most simply. Thus, we have overcome and therefore our victory stands firm on the word of Christ.

My dear reader, you see how neatly they take the words of Christ in their natural sense. Fool that I am, however, I wish to show in one small word this against those who as no Sacramentarians ever invert so great a statement and order of words of Christ and introduce a different meaning which does not and cannot exist in the words of Christ here. They are "Tutists," but for a different reason than those first Sacramentarians, for they have this dual "τοῦτο - this," something which they say the first holy fathers neglected and from which there followed the mistake which they are now correcting with this corrupted inversion of theirs, as if the fathers and we were unaware that it is one thing when Christ says: "This is My body," and another when He says: "Do this." Or as if the fathers were ignorant of allegories with which Origen and, after him, Jerome overflowed more than fairly often, or as if we are ignorant of allegories, even true ones provided in Scripture, or even those with which many people think that they are allowed to invent anything at all from anything at all whenever they wish.

Also, let us not say that our explanations are playing games with allegories, for they are merely abstaining from the word "allegory." Furthermore, as regards the matter itself, who doesn't see what they are doing? Even if they do not want to be "Significatists" (if this can happen), and even if they are unwilling to deal with allegories but say that they are presenting to us an image and the truth and that someone who was writing this passage about image and truth did this that he might say that there was no passage ever more necessary revealed in Scripture than that about image and truth; I say, if all this be true, what am I hearing? That the remission of sins and the eternal righteousness which is through Christ which have now been revealed through the grace of God our Father is far inferior to the passage about image and truth? Isn't this as if it be truly something new to say that material bread signifies spiritual bread or, that I may not sin against those who are unwilling to use the word "signifies," that the material bread is the image of that bread which is spiritual; for, just as that body, so also this one feeds the soul, etc.? What help does that rubbish provide as if it peddles some new revelation to the world so that you appear to be a new author?

"But," you say, "in this statement: 'The body of Christ is spiritual bread,' who denies that all the words are taken in their proper and natural significance?" But what does this have to do with the bread of the Supper in this inversion of those words? Briefly, they are unwilling to be "Significatists," as you have heard, nor do they wish to appear like the other Sacramentarians except in this alone: that they deny that the bread of the Lord and the cup of the Lord are the body and blood of Christ, something which we are asserting against them not because of the very elements of bread and wine, but because those are the words of Christ, etc.

What are they then? They certainly are absurd inverters of the words of Christ who take not even a single word (should you look at the statement and its way of thinking) in its proper and natural meaning. They make two changes (for we may now speak in this way): the one is a simple conversion: "The bread is My body" and "My body is bread"; here be careful not to say: "This bread." The other is an accidental one: "The bread is My body" and "My body is spiritual bread." And yet, if one were to change everything a thousand times, that consequence would not follow which they want us to infer by itself with such great sweat of their thinking processes, namely: "The bread of the Lord in the Supper is not His body." After all, that eternal truth which declares: "This bread which I am giving and distributing to you is My body. This cup which I am giving you to drink is My blood," remains forever.

We have said these things about their comparison by which they are comparing the Lord's Supper with John 6, and about the magnificent promise by which they promise that they wish to take here all the words of Christ in their natural sense. In my opinion, they already for a long time would have taken "this" for "such," so that "This," that is, "Some such thing is My body." This is something which squares not with the institution of Christ, but conforms very nicely with both their way of thinking and their inversion so that we can call them not "Tutists" but "Suchists," had they not feared that this very thing does not correspond sufficiently with their promise.

See now the rest of their words. They say: "We also divide the Lord's Supper into a spiritual eating and drinking and a worthy commemoration of breaking of bread and drinking of the Lord's cup, as Paul calls it."

They say these things in a quite confused fashion, just as those should say who either don't understand what they are saying or are unwilling to confess what they feel and take "breaking" for "eating." Otherwise, they would not say "the breaking of bread and the drinking of the Lord's cup." But I am tarrying too long here, and I don't want them thinking that I wish to bring up a false charge.

However, I wonder why they make the commemoration the same as the breaking or eating of the bread and the drinking of the cup when—both according to them and according to us—some people can take the bread and cup of the Lord without the remembrance, but badly—to their condemnation—against the command and institution of Christ. These things which can be separated are not the same, even if we have to connect them in the Lord's Supper (as I have also said earlier).

Moreover, what they say about spiritual eating and drinking, they say under a sacred appearance of truth, but with a double injury: one against the institution of Christ that the bread which we eat here corporally is not believed to be the body of Christ about which Christ nevertheless says: "This bread is My body." But if the fact that I say "This bread" displeases you, let what follows, namely: "This cup, etc.," not displease you. The other injury is against us, as if we are teaching that the corporal eating and drinking of this Sacrament occur without a spiritual eating and drinking, and that this is an external Sacrament (which contains within itself those things which the senses do not perceive but which Christ says) which we are to receive, absent faith. A short time ago some were trying to sow those lies among the common folk, but in vain, because our public writings and teaching contradict them.

Therefore, let them divide the Lord's Supper as they wish. We here are eating the Lord's body and drinking the Lord's blood in commemoration of Christ, just as we have said earlier and sufficiently about the bread and cup of the Lord.

However, they add: "In that remembrance, Christians are doing what Christ did and later what He commanded them to do in remembrance of Him, after He gave His body (on the cross) and shed His blood for the remission of sins, just as the Lord and Paul have expressed more broadly and quite clearly in their words."

I respond. You speak sacred words which are indeed sacred to us but not to you, for you adorn yourselves with that veneer that the common folk not believe that your way of thinking is contrary to the institution of Christ. Next, with these words (which otherwise are true among Christians), you are seeking to establish this lie of Satan that the bread of Christ is not the body of Christ and that the cup of Christ is not the blood of Christ, contrary to the obvious institution of Christ. Moreover, let me say that this bread of Christ or this cup of Christ is well-known from the words of Paul, who says: "This bread and cup of the Lord, etc.," namely, about which our Lord Jesus Christ declared: "This bread is My body, and this cup is My blood."

You say that these things have been said more broadly in the words of the Lord and of Paul that those who do not know the truth may in the meantime have wonderful feeling about you. If the things which they say have been expressed more broadly in the words of the Lord and of Paul, why are others contradicting them? Who contradicts the clear and expressed words of the Lord and of Paul without wickedness? Therefore we say that those matters have been expressed more broadly in the words of the Lord and of Paul, but not in your favor; for you have not yet introduced to us nor obliterated from us all the things which describe for us this sacred institution of Christ in such a way that we do not see what they wish.

With the same cover-up you often are mindful of the body of Christ which He surrendered on the cross and of His blood which He shed on the cross, not because we do not say that it is necessary to be mindful of them in the remembrance or announcement of His death, but because you are afraid that someone may feel badly about you in this way: "They speak many things about the

Lord's Supper. But why don't they speak about the body and blood of Christ?"

You say: "Christians do in their remembrance what Christ did and later commanded that they do, etc." No one denies this; but I do ask you who say these things: "When you say many things about doing what Christ commands, why don't you speak even once about believing what Christ says?" But that you not look for a place to flee to, I am speaking about faith in the words of Christ which He speaks in the Supper: "This bread is My body; this cup is My blood." Or have we not erred enough until now when we grasp at our works, but throw away the word of Christ? Where is your confession by which you confess that you are teaching many things about faith and the Spirit while in the meantime people have evil thoughts about us because of your words, as if we are teaching all things about the Sacrament without faith and as if we are asserting the truth of the words of Christ but denying the truth of the Christian faith?

On the basis of these words of yours, it follows that you are not Christians. You see, if those are Christians who do in this commemoration the things which Christ commands, you are not Christians. For when do you who do not believe what Christ says here do the things which Christ commands? Christ says: "This bread is My body; this cup is My blood." You do not believe that these words are true, but you still state that we must accept them in their proper and natural significance. Christ says: "...which is broken for you," but you cry out that the body of Christ is useless to us if it is in the bread. Therefore, when you deny in this way what Christ asserts in obvious language, what is that faith about which you are boasting? What confidence can you have in Christ, when you battle against the word of Christ?

He asserts, but you deny. He says: "He who is not with Me is against Me; and he who does not gather with Me, scatters." [Luke

11:23] However, because you do not believe what Christ says in this sacred institution, it necessarily follows that you are those very people who do not do what Christ commands you to do in this commemoration. After all, the Lord did not command: "Take and eat the bread which is not My body" just as you say that He commanded; but: "Take and eat the bread which is My body," for what else can you take from these words: "Take and eat. This bread is My body"? So, too, He did not command to drink the cup alone but the cup which is His blood. Just as you say, therefore, Christians here do what Christ commanded. They eat the body of the Lord believing that the bread which they eat is the Lord's body because of His word which says: "This is My body." They also drink the blood of the Lord believing His word which says: "This cup is My blood." Thus you are not doing what Christ commanded. In fact, with every effort and doctrine, you are even resisting that others do that [that is, keep Christ's word]. Where, then, is your Christianity in this area?

You cannot celebrate the Lord's Supper even if you come together a thousand times a day for your invented supper as if it were the Lord's Supper, because the institution of Christ does not recognize your bread and cup which you imagine you are receiving according to this command of Christ. Regardless of the name by which you call it, it is not what Christ instituted, but rather a human presumption as well as a manifest blasphemy against the word of Christ.

It is also worth our while to see what they add at the end of their confession, namely, the following words. They say: "As Christ instituted, Paul ordained for the Corinthians, the holy fathers observed in the primitive church; and Tertullian, Cyprian, Hilary, Augustine, and more wrote."

Here, if some quite learned person should press them hard as to what they want with those words: "As Christ instituted, etc.,"

for it appeared advisable to them to play around with that obfusca-
tion of theirs and to obscure the light, if that were possible; they will
respond: "First, we relate these words to those which immediately
preceded: 'As Christ instituted, the apostle ordained and the godly
preserved that those things be done in remembrance of Christ,' but
as if in the meantime there be someone who may deny this. Next,
we mention the holy fathers separately because the holy fathers
compared the Lord's Supper with John 6 that you may see with
what great holiness, learning, and authority the testimony for this
matter stands up for us that, when they wrote about John 6, they
wrote many things about the Sacrament of the Eucharist."

"And yet, who of us does not see what those unlearned
common folk are seeking to persuade with these words? Namely
this and nothing else. They all know that we perceive and teach that
the bread of the Lord's Supper in not the body of Christ nor is the
cup His blood. Therefore, when we burst forth with that conclu-
sion and awesome words: 'As Christ instituted, Paul ordained, etc.';
what else will the foolish common crowd which is utterly ignorant
of what we are saying think than that Christ, the apostles, all the
professors, and therefore all the godly have the same perceptions
that we have and therefore disdain those who teach that this bread
is the body of Christ and that this cup is the blood of Christ. In the
presence of the learned and of those who are pressing us hard we
therefore have something to respond."

However, to play around in so serious a matter is an indicator
of people who do not fear God—something which God has seen.

We therefore respond to those words in this way: No one
who may have wanted to see this institution which is described
with clear words in the evangelists and Paul can be ignorant of what
Christ instituted. Furthermore, if there are some who have been so
blinded by their own opinion against the very clear words of Christ
(however much they may boast of their own erudition), blindness

ought not accuse the very bright light of the sun. Who does not see in that ordination of Paul in 1 Corinthians what the apostles ordained, unless Paul is not an apostle and his arrangement is not apostolic? This is not to mention that when Christ at the Last Supper arranged and instituted this Sacrament of His body and blood and ordered that people do it in this way, he did not permit any apostle, any church, not even any angel, to change or arrange it differently, just as Paul says that the announcement of the Lord's death as often as we eat the bread and drink the cup of the Lord ought to continue in the Church of the faithful until He come (that is, until the last day of the world), even if the papists resist, even if the Sacramentarians resist, and anyone else resists in his own way.

If you wish to know what the apostle had to arrange, what the Church of God has to observe, what the teachers of the Church have to teach and write, and what all the faithful ought to perceive about this very sacred institution of the body and blood of Christ, where will you turn your eyes except to the very words of this institution and to the command of Christ? Who of the godly will approve anything against these words and command of Christ which were observed as expressed in this way and which have been taught and written elsewhere? Here no authority should take from us the authority of Christ about whom the Father said: "Listen to Him," and: "I shall be the avenger of him who does not listen." Also, Christ Himself says, John 12[:48]: "He who despises Me and does not accept My words has one to judge him. The word which I have spoken will judge him on the last day."

Do you want to know what authority the apostles alleged when they handed down to the churches of Christ this sacred institution of Christ? Listen to Paul as he says: "For I have received from the Lord what I also handed down to you, namely, that our Lord Jesus Christ in that night when He was betrayed, etc." [1 Cor. 12:23] Here he did not want to hand down (and ought not have handed down) anything other than what he had received from Christ, for he himself had written that it was required among stewards that a person be found faithful. [1 Cor. 4:2]

Therefore, along with the Church which we call "catholic" and "apostolic," which listens to Christ and does here just as Christ has instituted and commanded, we preserve whole and inviolate this institution of Christ, something which no gates of hell under any pretense up to this time could have persuaded us differently, now that the truth has been revealed. If some people teach and command otherwise, contrary to the institution of Christ, and in the meantime boast that they are the Church and that the Church can arrange differently, contrary to the arrangement and mandate of Christ, they will have seen that what they are saying certainly does not pertain to the catholic and apostolic Church which listens to Christ, at least in this case.

Next, to go further, what the holy fathers observed in addition in the primitive church again is well known from the [First] Epistle of Paul to the Corinthians, unless St. Paul, who was writing at that time to some people at Corinth and to whom he had preached, was not one of the holy fathers and did not belong to the primitive church. Give me some earlier and more ancient church which observed this institution of Christ differently or which believed that the bread of the Lord's Supper was not the body of the Lord. To what obscure places are you sending us when so great a light is present? If the discussion here involves the primitive church and what she observed—behold, you have the Corinthian Church which Paul established.

What fathers, then, are you raising as an objection to us contrary to Christ and to the apostles of Christ? Christians should accept apostolic teaching, which is the teaching of Christ. In fact, the sheep of Christ listen to the voice of their Shepherd. On the other hand, nothing pertains to them if any teachers under whatever disguise of Scripture or of holiness teach differently, for those sheep do not follow a stranger but flee from him, for they do not know the voice of strangers. The apostles set their doctrine atop the foundation, Christ. All other teachers from the apostles until the end of the world are bound by this precept, 1 Cor. 3[:10ff.]: "Let each see how he builds upon the foundation… that no godly teacher carelessly builds his teaching upon wood, hay, or stubble," that is, upon human foundations which are not the Word of God and which at some time must become confused and perish."For all flesh is as grass, and the glory of it is as the flower of the field, etc., but the word of the Lord will stand forever." [Isa. 40:6–7]

Those who want to be saints and teachers of the Church must themselves listen to Christ. Thus, they must present to us not what seems best to themselves, but what they have received from Christ, just as Paul said about this institution of Christ:"For I have received from the Lord what I have also handed down to you." [1 Cor. 10:23] Otherwise, tell me on what basis they could be called or be holy teachers?

Meanwhile, I am saying these things as if there are some of the ancient teachers who teach that the bread of the Lord's Supper is not the body of Christ and that the cup is not His blood. If they were to say this, they would be speaking not so much contrary to us as contrary to Christ, to Paul, and to the observance of the primitive church which you see among the Corinthians. Would a Christian listen to such things?

But now, because the ancients did not say this, why do we need to burden holy men with such unpopularity among Christians? Although they have understood some points in John 6 as references to the Sacrament of the bread and wine (something which we suffer as very troublesome, as I shall say later), nevertheless they have not said anything which could be contrary to us and in favor of those who deny that the bread in the Lord's Supper is the body of

Christ. In fact, they say in clear language what Christ says, namely, that the bread is the body of the Lord, and the cup His blood.

Therefore, although they may have used correctly or even abused the words of John 6 in favor of the Sacrament of the bread and wine; nevertheless, they speak in favor of us (namely, that which Christ institutes): that this bread is the body of Christ, and the cup His blood, because of the institution of Christ.

Because the learned and studious Oecolampadius was not ignorant of the reading of the ancients, namely, that the ancients interpreted some points of John 6 clearly as a reference to this Sacrament, I am surprised with what conscience he felt disparaged by some clear words of Chrysostom and thus dared to write and say: "Those who read these words of Chrysostom ought to remember to read his comments on John 6, where Christ says nothing about sacramental eating."

Let it be here that Christ is not speaking about sacramental eating (something which I think is true), nevertheless the fathers quite clearly said something there about sacramental eating and understood some words of Christ as references to the Sacrament of the bread and wine, something which Augustine says in this way at the beginning of Bk. 3 of his *de consensu evangelistarum*: "For those who were eating supper, etc." Moreover, John said nothing in this passage about the body and blood of the Lord, but bears clear witness that the Lord did speak in this way elsewhere in much greater detail. So much for Augustine.

"But," you say, "in their commentaries on John 6, the fathers say many things at the same time about the spiritual flesh and blood of Christ." And why not? What would they say there more appropriately? In addition, they do not deny that sacramental eating of the body of Christ which Christ instituted in the Supper. In fact, they confirm this in quite clear language. But the one without the other people do to their damnation, just as Paul also said.

However, let us hear the fathers themselves, whose names they themselves have expressed, that you may see what their perceptions are regarding this Sacrament of the bread and wine.

In his book *de resurrectione carnis*, Tertullian says that our flesh eats the body and blood of Christ, so that the soul, too, feasts on God. What could he say more clearly against the Sacramentarians? After all, he is speaking there about the Sacrament.

However, Cyprian (along with thirty-nine bishops) writes to Bishop Cornelius of Rome in this way, Bk. 1, *epistolae*, c. 2: "But now, peace is necessary not for the weak, but for the strong. We must give communion not to the dying, but to the living (He is saying these things about those who had denied Christ in time of persecution and who later repented and were ready to suffer for Christ.) that we may stir up and encourage them into battle. Let us not leave them naked and unarmed, but let us fortify them with the body and blood of Christ. When we administer the Eucharist for this purpose—that it can be the defense of those who receive it—let us arm those whom we want to be safe against our foe with the protection of the fullness of the Lord. After all, how can we call them forth to shed their blood in the confession of His name if we deny those soldiers the blood of Christ? Or how do we make them suitable for the cup of martyrdom if we do not first admit them to drink the cup of the Lord in the Church by right of communion?"

We have spoken these words in many ways against the Sacramentarians.

Hilary, *de trinitate*, Bk. 8, speaks in this way: "If the Word truly became flesh, and if we truly receive the Word made flesh in the Lord's Supper, how must we consider that it does not remain naturally within us? For He was born a man and assumed the nature of our flesh which is now inseparable from Him. He now mixes the nature of His flesh into the nature of eternity under the Sacrament of flesh to be shared with us." Again: "If, then, Christ truly took on the flesh of our body, and if that man who was born of Mary is truly Christ; we truly receive the flesh of His body under a mystery, and in this way we shall become one, etc."

I spoke earlier about Augustine.

Therefore, because such great men have spoken in this way on behalf of the word of Christ, why do we now cause them to become infamous as if, when Christ says: "This is My body," they themselves said: "This is not Your body"? That I now not repeat that, even if the fathers had written in favor of the Sacramentarians (something which they didn't do, and if some of their more obscure words seem to have drawn you to that point, see what they say elsewhere in more clear and lucid words); I say, had they written in favor of the Sacramentarians, this sacred institution of Christ still should remain unharmed for Christians, preserved as it was under the apostles in the primitive church.

Now finally I am of the opinion that you do see what those Sacramentarians want for themselves when against all other Sacramentarians they promise that they want to accept all the words in their proper and natural meanings when Christ says: "This is My body, etc." To make us submit to themselves, and yet, to not depart from the Sacramentarians, they deny that this bread is the body of the Lord and the cup His blood. They are not so much comparing (as they falsely promise) the Lord's Supper with John 6 as, rather, inverting the words of Christ that people may take them in a distorted way and subvert this entire institution of Christ. Their playing with allegories and empty human inventions ought not take from us the truthfulness of Christ's words.

I have said these things more freely about these Sacramentarians than about others, not only because the others are more well known from their public writings than that there is a need to disclose what they want, but also because these about whom I have been speaking now are in the habit of admonishing us both through letters which they have sent and in our presence by their speech. They are also in the habit of swearing by the terrifying judgment of God and all the sacred things of Christians that, if we should see them make any mistake, we should indicate that—something which I see they even now are demanding in their public writing which I wish those who have written would have published not under an alias but under their own name.

Look, I have provided what I could if I have gained as my brothers those who listen to me. God and my Lord Jesus Christ are my witnesses that I believe that I have spoken the truth. I cannot defect from the sure words of Christ and this institution which Matthew, Mark, Luke, and Paul have written and go to the empty fictions of men and the wavering opinions of those who despise the word of Christ. Our salvation must be dearer to us than that we embrace uncertain human words instead of the absolutely certain and indubitable words of Christ.

However, they may have despised me as unlearned and crude as if I not understand their spirituality because of my carnality; inflated as they are by these prideful words and because of the ignorance of their carnal mind about the things which they are affirming, they generally are cheered up against us. Meanwhile, with their fearful consciences (which I do not doubt they have) telling them that God and the ministers of the Word of God nevertheless are not ultimately going to suffer such things; I shall comfort myself and sing with the psalmist, saying: "Then they will be most fearful because the Lord is in the generation of the just person. You have put to shame the counsel of the humble or despised man because the Lord is his refuge." [Psa. 14:4–5] In this case, my confidence is in these words because I am asserting nothing against the Lord and His Christ, for I, sinner that I am, am giving glory to the word and institution of my Lord, Jesus Christ.

However, if my adversaries may have complained that I have said some things too harshly (as they generally do when they are unwilling to yield to the truth), they should know that I should not have adorned their wicked teaching with good words.

However, when I see that they have abused John 6 in their teaching, I assumed from this that they deny the sacred institution of Christ about this Supper, that is, that they claim that the bread of the Lord is not the body of the Lord and that the cup of the Lord is not His blood, something which no one of the ancients ever did, for they have used some words from John 6 in favor of this institution and not against it, as we have said earlier. I shall tell my way of thinking about John 6. No one should be annoyed at me if he may understand some things to be in favor of this Sacrament, just as some of the ancients understood some things. After all, we are not condemning things which they said in a godly and true way even if they said them at times out of place, provided you not abuse them by claiming a falseness which is contrary to the truthfulness of God, as I now see that those Sacramentarians are doing.

First, in John 6 we have the narrative of the feeding of the crowd with a few loaves and fishes. Next, when the crowd sought Jesus, they heard: "Amen. Amen. I say to you, you are seeking Me not because you have seen miracles but because you ate of the loaves and were filled. Do not work for the food that perishes, etc." [v. 26–27] On the basis of this passage, He is warning them not to seek food to fill the belly but spiritual food from which to have eternal life. The Son of God, who took on flesh and blood on our behalf, is this food. Therefore He calls Himself "the Bread which has come down from heaven." He also says that the glorious manna of the Jews scarcely was a shadow of this true Bread or heavenly Manna.

Furthermore: "Eat this bread," or, as He says later: "Eat this flesh of the Son of God and drink this blood of the Son of God by faith," that you may have therefrom not fullness of your belly for an hour but eternal life, clearly, that you may eat forever in a spiritual way the flesh of the Son of God and drink the blood of the Son of

God, that is, that you be incorporated with the very Son of God or Christ, who is both God and man (because God and man in that Person of Christ cannot be separated from each other), until you do not stop believing He became flesh and blood for you, that is, became true man, giving up the same flesh and blood for you on the cross, and until you do not believe or hope for salvation or eternal life in anyone else but that one incarnate Son of God.

To believe eternally, therefore, is forever to eat and drink spiritually the flesh and blood of Christ, the Son of God, to be united with and incorporated into Christ. From this, it happens that you cannot help but have eternal life because the incarnate Son of God to whom you are united by faith can only be eternal life so that He Himself, who has cleansed and sanctified His bride, can say about her: "This now is bone of My bones and flesh of My flesh," something which you see in Eph. 5, just as He says here: "He who eats My flesh and drinks My blood remains in Me and I in him. As the living Father has sent Me, and as I live because of the Father; so he who has eaten Me himself will live because of Me" [v. 56–57]; and: "He therefore has eternal life, and I shall raise him on the last day." [v. 54]

This which I have said is the sense of the words of Christ and of that entire discourse; namely, that Christ is teaching and commending there faith or trust in the incarnate Christ or in the flesh and blood of Christ which is not flesh like the sinful flesh of men but the flesh of the Son of God, nor is His blood like the blood of others but the blood of the Son of God. This is what the words of the entire discourse of Christ declare very obviously. In this way, you see that by the eating of Christ's flesh and drinking of His blood nothing else is being commended there but faith in the incarnate Christ, the very Mediator between God and man, the very crucified Christ whom God made for us wisdom, righteousness, sanctification, and redemption, that he who boasts may boast in the

Lord, because the Father sent Him forth for us that He might be our mercy-seat through faith in His blood.

Without faith it is a pure lying hypocrisy if you should say that you believe in God, the Creator of heaven and earth, just as the Jews are now presuming to whom Christ once said: "You say that God is your Father, and you don't know Him; but I know Him, and if I should have said that I don't know Him, I shall be a liar like you." [John 8:55] For who can believe in Him or have trust in Him who you—burdened in your conscience as you are with your sins—think is an angry Judge, when the matter is under serious discussion? You will rather flee from His sight, as the Jews did on Horeb. Moreover, you will approach the Father at the time when you know by faith His Only-Begotten, who was handed over for you. Through this faith you now have a good conscience about the forgiveness of sins and you are reconciled to God. You will therefore also know that you have become a child of God, something which He says elsewhere: "I am the way, the truth, and the life. No one comes to the Father except through Me." [John 14:6]

Here God is my witness as to how I shrink from the wicked dogma of Zwingli that, from the fact that he makes original sin not a damnable sin but a sort of defect and from the fact that he recently taught in a public writing that we must take the words of Christ: "My flesh is truly food," in this way: "My flesh, that is, My divinity, which, even as the flesh of Christ, cannot truly nourish anyone," because the flesh of Christ (according to Him) cannot benefit anyone.

However, if wickedness can accuse me falsely as cursed as if on the basis of Scripture I am trusting in man and placing strength in my arm; I respond that he is cursed and anathema who does not understand those and similar words in Scripture as references to that Man who is God, as references to that flesh which is the flesh of the Son of God, as references to His blood which is the blood of the Son of God, because the Word was made flesh. But blessed is he and he has eternal life who (along with the prophets and holy apostles and all the elect) confesses from his heart that the blessing is given to all nations in the very Seed of Abraham; that is, Christ Jesus, our Lord, the Son of God, who was crucified for us. This is the Man who is God, this is the flesh which is the flesh of the Son of God. "There is salvation in no other, nor has any other name been given under heaven to men in whom we must be saved." [Acts 4:12] Cursed therefore is that person who does not trust in that Man Christ, who is God, who goes not put aside that flesh of Christ, which flesh is the flesh of the Son of God, His arm. The wickedness of people will not divide that unity of the one Person in Christ after the Word became flesh with such great esteem.

In fact, let us run through the words of the discourse of Christ from beginning to end so that you may see that He is teaching nothing else here than what I have said; namely, that faith in the incarnate Son of God, that is, our incorporation into Him under the figurative words of "eating" and "drinking," by which Christ Himself nevertheless explained with such clear language in so long a discourse what they intend, to wit, that there is no need to listen to another schoolmaster. We are presenting to you what you are seeking—what the words of our Master want here, and the interpretation thereof of the same Master.

He says [v. 27]: "Do not work for the bread which perishes but for that which endures to eternal life, which the Son of Man will give you, for God the Father has sealed Him." He calls Himself "food," namely, the Son of God in the flesh, something which He will declare later with many clear words that we not hold in contempt that humanity and incarnation of the Son of God in such a way that we dare to say about these wickedly and blasphemously along with some people: "The flesh of Christ provides no benefit." You will see clearly here that declaration of Paul: "We preach Christ crucified, an offense to the Jews and foolishness to the Gentiles, but to those who have been called, both Jews and Gentiles, Christ, the power of God, etc." [1 Cor. 1:23–24]

This food endures to eternal life not only for him but also for us, for He says these things for our benefit. After all, He alone is the food of eternal life, that is, the food from which we receive and have eternal life and are absolved from eternal death (as you will see later). Food for the body perishes and is of service to one who is perishing. However, this food does not perish but preserves the person who eats it to eternal life, for He is eternal life, as He says elsewhere: "I am the way, the truth and the life" [John 14:6]; and again: "This is eternal life, that they may know You, the only true God, and Him whom you have sent, Jesus Christ." [John 17:3]

Because He said: "Work for this food"; no one take this to mean that someone by his own effort or zeal or merit can prepare this food for himself, for He adds: "The Son of Man will give you this food." Unless He Himself grants that you believe in that incarnate Son of God Himself, you will never believe but will forever remain an offense and foolishness for yourself. You will remain hungry and dried out so that, even if you hear and read the reason for that faith, swollen as you are in the mind of your flesh, you will say: "The flesh of Christ does not provide any benefit. It is enough for me to believe in God, the Creator of heaven and earth, who led our fathers out of Egypt, etc. Thus, I do not have in addition some crucified God who was unable to help Himself, etc.," just as the Jews say today.

The hypocrite does not see that this is not true when he says that he believes in God, the Creator of heaven and earth, as Christ says elsewhere: "No one comes to the Father except through Me" [John 14:6]; and again: "No one knows the Father except the Son and him to whom the Son wanted to reveal Him." [Mat. 11:27] Also, John the Baptist says: "No one has ever seen God. The only begotten Son, who is in the bosom of the Father, has Himself told of Him." [John 1:18]

But, when the Son of Man will have given us this food (that is, when He will have given that we be incorporated by faith into Himself), then we labor for this food, for you cannot work for it before you have or receive it. Then in all temptations exercise yourselves in that faith against sin, death, and Satan that you may grow in a holy increase in the Lord. Also preach it to others and among yourselves that others may be incorporated into the incarnate Son of God and be in the one body of Christ along with you. From this faith will also follow other fruits of good works for your neighbors. Preach it also that you may suffer for Christ just as He suffered for you. This, you see, is to work for this food after you will have received it from the Son of Man.

I have no doubt but that, when Christ speaks about faith here, He used the word "labor" because He was speaking to the self-righteous Jews who were not walking in the footsteps of the holy prophets. Therefore they could conceive of no righteousness except that righteousness of their own works which does not justify before God. Although He may be summoning them away from this opinion with these words: "…which the Son of Man will give you"; nevertheless, as if they didn't hear Him (as happens to those whose opinions have blinded them), they immediately ask Him about His own works and say [v. 28]: "What shall we do that we may work the works of God, that is, the works which God wants us to do?" This is as if they are saying: "…provided you have said nothing so difficult but that we may do it."

It is amazing with what skill He here depicts how we all have been so influenced because of our nature to feel in favor of the righteousness of the flesh against the righteousness of God which alone justifies, that is, which removes sin and grants eternal life. This is the righteousness of Christ.

Moreover Jesus responds [v. 29]: "This is the work of God," that is, what God wants us to do, namely, "that you believe in Him

whom He has sent," that is, in the incarnate Son of God. Therefore
He mentions His sending that you may understand that He has
become flesh. After all, it is not unclear to Christians how the Son
of God was sent to us and came; to wit, He became the Son of Man
or put on our flesh or, as John says, became flesh. Therefore He also
mentions later His descent from heaven because He was sent from
heaven to be among us and appeared in His true flesh, "because the
Word was made flesh and lived among us, and we have seen His
glory, etc." [John 1:14]

He was not made flesh in such a way that He stopped being God, but He is now God in such a way that He is also Man; for,
if God were that Son of Man who came down from heaven as the
Father had sent Him, He would not say that He was going to give
the food of eternal life and that He Himself was that food. That
Son of Man, therefore, is the food of eternal life and thus is eternal
life, because He is at the same time both God and Man. You see, if
He were Man alone, where would our mediator between God and
man be? Or, if He were only God, where would our mercy-seat in
His blood be? Here by the highest right He would have been able
to call Himself the Son of God, but He said that He was the Son of
Man that you might see what He has become for you and to what
this entire cause which He is pleading leads.

But that we not despise Him because He is the Son of
Man, He declares that He is God when He says that He is going
to give this food, that is, that He is going to grant that we believe in
Him. This is because He gives the Holy Spirit for the preaching of
the Gospel by which we believe in Christ and through Christ are
certain that we have the Father kindly-disposed toward us that we
may call upon Him with confidence.

Not only is He as Man eternal life, and not only is He as
God eternal life for us or that food, but it has pleased God that
Christ the Lord, that is, that He, who is at the same time God and

Man, was crucified for us as our wisdom, righteousness, sanctification, and eternal life, something which He added when He said: "... for God the Father sealed this Son of Man. You hear the Son of Man and God the Father so that you also believe that the Son of God is this Son of Man."

Thus, I am repeating in detail as Christ also certainly is repeating this against those who today are saying in detail that there is one Person in Christ, God and Man. Furthermore, they actually are separating them, as far as their teaching is concerned, for they are teaching that the flesh of Christ is not of any benefit and that what is said about the flesh of Christ (namely, that it is truly food), we must take as a reference not to His flesh but to His divinity, as I said earlier.

He says: "God the Father sealed this Son of Man." God wanted all the treasures of wisdom and knowledge to be sealed and hidden in this Son of Man or in this Man. You will have sought in vain for wisdom elsewhere that you may know what pleases God and what displeases Him. The same is true of the knowledge that you may know that God is your Father. You will have sought in vain the remission of sins or the righteousness of God and eternal life elsewhere. For God sealed Him that all the fullness of His deity might dwell bodily in this propitiation. Look for God there. It is there that He dwells. You will have sought the Father elsewhere in vain. He says: "He who sees Me, also sees My Father. Do you not believe that I am in the Father and that the Father is in Me?" [John 14:9–10]

Up to this point, therefore, Christ has been proposing that we have a need for God, namely, to believe in Him as incarnate, as I have said; for without this all our works and efforts are nothing before God. This faith incorporates us with Christ so that He who is our food and from whom we have eternal life dwells in us and we in Him, as He says later. Moreover, the words which follow are an explanation of these [points].

Therefore, I do not think it necessary to indicate in greater detail about what food Christ says this, after you have heard from His mouth: "Labor for the food which does not perish, etc. This is the work of God that you believe in Him whom He has sent." You have the work of God and eternal life, if you believe in the incarnate Son of God.

However, it is worthwhile to see here how the natural man or the flesh (that is, man without the Spirit) does not understand the things which are of God, so that Christ does not later say in vain [v. 63]: "It is the Spirit who gives life. The flesh is of no benefit." As often as you now hear the Jews debating, arguing, and murmuring against these words of Christ so that they finally become offended and depart from Him, so often will you hear nothing other than the flesh, that is, people without the Spirit, who cannot believe the words of Christ.

But as often as you hear Christ speaking, you will hear the Spirit of God, just as He says [v. 63]: "The words which I have spoken to you are Spirit and life." These words are Spirit and life for you if you believe, just as He adds [v. 64]: "But there are some of you who do not believe." Peter says [v. 68]: "Lord, to whom shall we go? You have the words of eternal life, and we believe and know that you are the Christ, the Son of the living God." From these words, you see what He is calling "Spirit and life," namely, to believe and trust Christ according to this discourse of Christ, for these are the words of the Spirit and of eternal life so that you have no doubt what He is saying is the flesh is when He says: "The flesh is of no benefit," namely, that killing and destroying or damning flesh which He opposes to the life-giving Spirit, that same flesh which does not know how to believe the words of Christ but rather takes offense because of them and receives poison and death from the Word—from which same Word believers receive the Holy Spirit and eternal life. That's how far the flesh is from being of no benefit!

We judge as accursed those who say here that Christ is saying that His flesh is of no benefit, although He nevertheless said earlier that it gives life to the world and that there cannot be life for the world without it. Here, you see, He is not saying: "My flesh is of no benefit," nor is He speaking about His own flesh and blood as He was earlier, but about the Spirit and the flesh. He is opposing the life-giving Spirit to the flesh which is of no benefit, that is undoubtedly, the damned and damning flesh. The flesh cannot comprehend the words of the Spirit but is offended, murmurs against them and blasphemes. Briefly, it does not believe. The Spirit in the believing disciples says: "You have the words of eternal life, and we believe, etc."

Moreover, we do not judge as cursed, but rather that those have spoken in a godly way, although perhaps not in the right place, who have interpreted this very thing about the Sacrament of the Eucharist from the ancient and the modern writers. They say: "The flesh of Christ in the Sacrament which people eat only carnally is of no benefit. In fact, according to Paul, they eat it to their judgment. It is, however, of much benefit, that is, it is received to eternal life, if the life-giving Spirit be present, that is, if you should receive the Sacrament not just with your mouth as the unworthy receive it, but also with faith, that is, trusting in the flesh and blood of the Son of God, something which is called 'eating spiritually.'" Nevertheless they are not denying a physical eating of the body of Christ in the Sacrament through this. Who would condemn these godly words, however much people might not be saying them in the right place? But, if some people should later abuse them to deny some truth of God, who would approve them?

Where now are those who promise to prove from the context that which Christ says here: "The flesh is of no benefit" is to be understood simply as that the very flesh of Christ is of no benefit, and is not the life of the world, but which is flesh not as of others but as of the Son of God, as we have said? In themselves, the flesh of Christ and the words which He speaks about His flesh certainly are Spirit and life, but they are of no benefit to you just as they are of no benefit to Satan, because you do not believe that that flesh is your salvation, as you have heard from Christ. Therefore you would also say in a godly manner about the flesh of Christ that it is outside the reckoning of the external Sacrament, namely, that it is of no benefit to you without the Spirit, that is, without faith, that is, unless you believe, just as the whole Trinity is of no benefit to you without the Spirit, that is, unless you believe. Augustine brings out a simile and says from Paul: "Knowledge inflates. Now then, should we hate knowledge? Heaven forbid! Add charity which edifies, and knowledge will be of benefit and will not inflate." Thus, the flesh of Christ is useful for you if the Spirit has been present, that is, if you believe. People can say such and similar things in a godly way and not contrary to the reckoning of our faith however much out of place they may be.

Therefore we must explain what is said simply; namely, that the flesh of Christ is useless. "My flesh truly is food, and My blood truly is drink." That is, My divinity is truly food and drink which feed for eternal life. It is not my humanity nor my flesh and blood but is clearly of that spirit which destroyed Jesus and which has no commerce with these words of Christ which are Spirit and life for the believer. You see, it is the spirit of the Antichrist which does not confess that Jesus Christ came in the flesh, for to say that the flesh of Christ is of no benefit and to say that it is nothing or does not exist is to say the same thing.

Therefore you have something which you can otherwise say in a godly way, if the sure way of thinking of this passage which we have said is not pleasing but you nevertheless may not subvert it here.

With these words, therefore, I have indicated my way of thinking about John 6, namely, that there does occur that eating of the food or heavenly bread, that is, the eating of the body and drinking of the blood of the incarnate Son of God which includes faith in the incarnate Son of God by which it happens that we are united with Him and grow into Him.

However, if there is someone so senseless that he desires me to indicate this statement in individual words which I have omitted to do in the midst of this consultation, I am quite willing to be of such service even to him.

That flesh or human hypocrisy which asks: "What do we do to perform the works of God?," seems to be willing to follow if it have heard the will of God, for in the meantime, it dreams to itself (as always) that Christ or the Gospel is going to prescribe not a different righteousness than one of external works. However, when it hears that this demands faith in Christ, when the response comes: "This is the work of God that you believe in Him whom He has sent," it does not accept the truth and does not begin to believe these words but struggles and argues against them.

Therefore they say: "What miracle are You performing? Moses fed our fathers with heavenly manna in the wilderness," as if to say that Moses by a great miracle fed the fathers living things for the belly (who seek Christ not because they saw miracles by which to believe but because they ate of His bread and fishes). "If You were to feed us lazy people in similar fashion or even better, absent our labor, why wouldn't we prefer You? Otherwise we don't see what we should accept greatly in You ahead of others."

He begins to strengthen them with an oath undoubtedly that the faithful may believe this discourse, even if all the rest be offended and depart from the Gospel. He says [v. 32]: "Amen. Amen. I say to you, Moses did not give you the bread from heaven that you may prefer him to Me, for He was a servant of God through whom God showed wonderful things to your fathers. My Father, however, who gave that manna, a corruptible food, to satisfy the belly at that time is now giving you true bread from heaven, that is, His incarnate Word if you believe, eat, and are fed." You see, the bread of God is that which God Himself and not Moses gives. It is the bread which comes down from heaven and gives life to the world, that is, to ruined and condemned people.

With these words, He commends the grace of God and excludes human merit. He says: "The Father gives not to the saints but to the world," but in such a way that those who receive it no longer remain the world, that is, the kingdom of Satan and of the wicked, just as He says about His disciples: "They are in the world but they are not of the world." [John 15:19] Furthermore, He is calling them away from Moses to Himself, away from the righteousness of the Law to the righteousness of God, which is Himself through whom alone we who believe are justified.

For these matters you will observe what I said earlier. The Son of Man, who gives you this food, is now saying: "My Father is giving you the true bread from heaven." He speaks in this way elsewhere about the Comforter: "…whom I shall send you and whom the Father will send in My name," [John 14:16 and 26] that you may see that the Father and the Son have the same divine power and that both are giving the Holy Spirit by which you may believe in Christ for eternal salvation."

That you not despise the flesh of Christ as if it offers no benefit, He does not say: "The Son of God will give you this food," but "the Son of Man." Thus, you see that this Son of Man is truly God because He gives you this food of eternal life, as the Father does from heaven. He says: "You do not believe that I am in the Father and the Father is in Me." [John 10:38]

I indeed am not unaware that there are in Christ two natures, one divine and the other human, and that the latter is not the former. However, I confess that, according to the Gospel, these two natures are connected in Christ in such a unity of the Person that they cannot be separated so that God is man and man is God, or the Word is flesh and the flesh is Word. Therefore I say this about the whole Person not only with words which otherwise don't fit both natures separately but actually and really. Thus Christ, who is not only man alone or God alone but God and man simultaneously, is born, preaches, performs miracles, dies, rises again, and has power in heaven and on earth.

Scripture speaks in this way that "God did not spare His own Son but gave Him up for us all." [Rom. 8:32] The Son of God has this property that, if He were not man, He would not die; but if He were man alone, His death would be of no benefit to me. Therefore, I am redeemed by the death of the Son of God, as Paul says, Acts 20[:28]: "God purchased the Church with His own blood," because that man who died for me is the Son of God and God Himself.

Here, then, the Son of Man is not only said to give, but truly does give the food of eternal life. In this way, He Himself is the food because He Himself is God and His flesh is the flesh of the Son of God and His blood is the blood of the Son of God. God is in that flesh and in that blood as He reconciles the world to Himself. His nature, therefore, is that life-giving flesh and that life-giving blood, however much it does not benefit the unbelieving who, when they hear the Word of God about that flesh and blood, are offended, and go away.

Therefore, when they hear that the bread which is to be given from heaven is much better than manna and respond [v. 34]: "Lord, give us that bread forever," they take that to mean bread for the belly. Already for a long time, their spirit has been in their dishes, and they cannot dream of a different flesh other than the righteousnesses of the flesh and the conveniences of this life.

Hear here how clearly He is saying that food and drink are faith in Himself incarnate. He says [v. 35]: "I am the bread of life. He who comes to Me (obviously by faith) will not hunger; and he who believes in Me will never thirst; that is, he will require nothing other than Me for righteousness and eternal life. Without the Word of God, he will be fouled by every human righteousness and whatever people call 'divine.' But he who will have faith in Me alone will have enough." [v. 36] "But I have spoken to you who have even seen Me and have not believed. This celestial food therefore is not your food for life but more for death because you were not content with the present food which was offered you by the word of preaching. What excuse do you have? You have seen miracles, you have eaten of My bread and fishes, and yet you have not believed. Were you to believe in Him whom the Father sent, you would perceive a different refreshment, namely, that you had been freed from your sins, that you were the children of God, and that you had eternal life so that you might call upon the Father with the greatest confidence."

Because one might have this faith and eat the bread of life or drink the drink of life and for this reason attribute something to his own effort and free will (just as we said before), He adds [v. 37]: "Everything which the Father gives to Me will come to Me, and Him who comes to Me I am not casting out." First, He commends grace over against merit and human boasting and says: "Everything which the Father gives to Me will come to Me, that is, it cannot happen that those whom the Father predestined would be Mine not come to Me," just as Paul says, Eph. 1[:4]: "God has chosen us in Christ before the foundations of the world were laid." What merits were ours before we existed, in fact, when the world still did not exist?

Next, He offers great comfort to those who have already come to Christ, that is, who already believe in Christ according to the Gospel, as we expressed earlier what it means to come to Him. He comforts them and says: "Him who comes to Me I am not casting out." But what else does this mean other than that those who believe (that is, who seriously seek salvation in Christ), cannot be damned? That the Father has given or predestined to Christ those who believe is a most certain sign to them that they have accepted the Gospel and believe in Christ seriously. No more certain sign can our spirit have than that God the Holy Spirit has sealed us to believe in Christ, for "the Spirit of God bears witness to our spirit that we are the children of God." [Rom. 8:16]

However, those who believe for a time and in time of temptation depart because they have taken offense at the Gospel or at Christ have not believed seriously but either were being held by some opinion or were seeking their own advantage under the name of Christ, just as did those Capernaites, about whom John also speaks in c. 2[:23]: "Many believed in His name when they saw the miracles which He was performing, but Jesus would not entrust Himself to them because He knew all men, etc."

The elect can err temporarily and, even feeling abandoned by God, they can deny Him as did Peter. However, those who have erred are always ready to have the Word of God instruct them. Those who deny Him immediately return to Him, for they know that there is no salvation beside faith in Christ, just as He said to Peter: "Peter, I have prayed for you that your faith not fail, etc." [Luke 22:32] Furthermore, offended as they are, the wicked depart from the Word which they seemed to have accepted, just as those Capernaites, so that they never wish to return. They have no awareness of having denied the truth so that they repent or desire forgiveness but rather grieve and disdain faith because they have clung to that opinion and sect (for that's they way they feel). Later, they resist very strongly the preaching of the truth. The world today is filled with these examples. John says about these [1.2:19]: "Those Antichrists have departed from us, for, had they been of us, they surely would have remained with us, etc."

Therefore, he who seeks his salvation in Christ seriously, according to the Gospel, should give thanks to the Father of mercies, for he has an absolutely certain sign of his election, strengthened as he is through this word: "Him who cometh to Me I am not casting out." He does not give us His word in vain. Through that Christ of His, how has He not with Him given us all things?

To this sure comfort of believers in Christ also pertain the things which follow. He says [v. 38]: "Because I came down from heaven, etc.," for weaker consciences are confused and say: "I am a sinner, but Christ is the judge of the living and the dead. Not only as judge but also as just, He cannot endure what is unjust; how, then, shall I hope for salvation through Him?" Here Christ comforts and says: "Although by right My will would be to destroy the unjust and sinners, My Father also has this will. Were I to wish to act according to My right and not be merciful, My Father, nevertheless, because of My mission and My coming down from heaven, that is, because of My incarnation and ministry on earth, now wants something else until the day of the final judgment. Because He wants that, I must want it and I even do want it." [v. 39]: "This is the will of My Father, who has sent Me, that I not lose anything of all that He has given Me but that I raise it again on the last day," that it may appear that they have not lost their life even because of physical death. In the meantime, they are sleeping in Christ. [v. 40:] "This is the will of Him that sent Me that everyone who sees the Son and believes in Him may have eternal life," and not be thought to have lost his life in the body. "I shall raise him on the last day." He also speaks in this way in John 3[:16–17]: "God so loved the world that He gave His only-begotten Son that everyone who believes in Him not perish but have eternal life, for God did not send His Son into the world to condemn the world but to save the world through Him, etc."

Here the flesh or human reason does not restrain itself but disdains the Son of Joseph for promising such wonderful things about Himself. To them, He says, despite their ingratitude, [v. 43]: "Don't murmur among yourselves to increase your sins. The flesh cannot understand what I am saying. You need the Spirit to believe, and God gives that Spirit. Here your wisdom or free will are nothing. It is impossible for anyone to come to Me, that is, to believe in Me, unless the Father, who sent Me, that is, who wanted Me to become incarnate, has drawn him with His Spirit by revealing to him the Gospel to believe, and I shall raise him on the last day."

Furthermore, the Father draws by teaching outwardly with the ministry of external preaching and internally with His anointing or Spirit. Otherwise, when would the flesh grasp the words of the Spirit and of life, as it written in Isa. 54? They will all be in a new kingdom, that is, in the kingdom of Christ, where God will teach them. Here, as He says, the Father draws, so He says elsewhere that He, the Crucified, is going to draw. He says: "And I, if I shall have been lifted up from the earth, shall draw all things to Myself." [John 12:32] He says "all," that is, "not only Jews but also Gentiles, to whom through the ministry of the Spirit, that is, through the preaching of the Gospel, I shall grant that they believe in Me, for then they will be unable not to cling to Me." In the meantime, this is what it means to be drawn by the Father or by Christ, namely, to be taught in this way by the Spirit.

[v. 45]: "Everyone, therefore, who has heard of the Father," that is, who has heard the Word of God even by external preaching, etc. I am expressing this because there are those who from these and similar passages despise the Word of God as it is preached or written externally because of their "spirituosity," as if Christ Himself is not offering this long discourse in external words which even the wicked Capernaites are hearing but, as He Himself is saying, that these are Spirit and life to those who believe, that is, that this is being said to the disciples of God, just as Peter declares, [v. 68]: "Lord, to whom shall we go? You have the words of eternal life, and we believe, etc." The Word, when preached externally, not only does not benefit those who hold it in contempt but even makes them worse. Nevertheless it does benefit those who receive it, for the ministry of the Spirit is the external preaching of the Gospel, or as Paul says, "the ministry [223] of reconciliation" [2 Cor. 5:18] by which it happens that we are reconciled to God if we believe the preaching which, through the preaching of the apostles, reveals to us about Christ "the things which eye does not see nor ear heard nor have risen in the heart of man," [1 Cor. 2:9] namely, "the wisdom hidden from the ages." [1 Cor. 2:7]

He therefore not only said: "Everyone who has heard of the Father," but He also added: "...and learned [of Him]"—for many hear of the Father, for the word of the Father is the Gospel, when it is preached externally. Nevertheless they do not learn, as happened in the case of the Capernaites, that is, they are not the disciples of the Schoolmaster, Christ. You see, they despise this Schoolmaster because He does not teach what they themselves are prescribing.

Lest anyone say here: "If one learns from the Father, the Father therefore is seen, which is contrary to Scripture which says [v. 46]: 'No one has seen the Father except Him who is of God; He has seen the Father.'" With these words, He is denying to all people who do not learn of God a knowledge of God the Father. They indeed speak many things about God, but they don't know Him. Those, however, know Him who entertain no doubts but that He is their Father and that they are His children. By what means do they know this? Who knows the mind of the Lord? He says: "He who is of God, that is, the Son, sees the Father, and He can reveal the Father to us." Otherwise, all human wisdom is foolishness, and all righteousness is sin. John the Baptist speaks in this way in John 1[:18]: "No one has ever seen God. The only-begotten Son, who is in the bosom of the Father, has told us of God" or the Father through the Gospel, that we may see by faith through grace the Father who otherwise is invisible to all because of our blindness. Christ says elsewhere: "No one knows the Father except the Son and him to whom the Son was willing to reveal Him." [Mat. 11:27]

You see again here that the Father reveals and the Son reveals internally, otherwise undoubtedly no differently than through the Holy Spirit, and externally through the ministry of the Holy Spirit that you may see that in the divine Trinity there is one will and one operation.

However, He continues His discourse with the following very clear words [v. 47–51]: "Amen. Amen. I say to you, he who believes in Me has eternal life. I am that bread of life. Your fathers ate manna in the wilderness and died"—many of them not so much a physical as an eternal death. (See the account in 1 Cor. 10.) "This is that bread which comes down from heaven that a person may eat of it and not die. I am the living bread which has come down from heaven. If anyone will have eaten of this bread, he will live forever."

That no one may despise the flesh of Christ as something which is of no benefit, He explains Himself and says [v. 51b]: "The bread which I shall give you is My flesh. I shall give this bread for the life of the world. I shall give it on the cross where the treasure of human salvation is. Later I shall give it for the whole world. That is, I shall distribute it throughout the world with the preaching of the Gospel that whoever will have believed the preached Gospel may have that treasure and become incorporated into Me for eternal life."

Let us speak here about those who had pretended for the sake of their belly and their own advantages that they were the disciples of Christ, of which pretense and hypocrisy the world is filled. When it is necessary for them to thank the Schoolmaster for having expressed Himself so clearly about faith in His incarnation and to implore Him to deign to teach them the things they were not understanding, they begin to rage like madmen all the more in the wisdom of their own flesh and say: "How can He here give us His flesh to eat?" They accuse Him of lying, and their foolish reason does not see that He is not some deceiver who was performing such great miracles which no one can do unless God has been with him. That you may see their terrible blindness, they themselves had eaten of the bread and fishes and not only had been present at, but even had been part of, the miracle. Therefore, they should not have doubted His words regardless of how greatly they were unable to understand them.

Christ, however, offended on the basis of His word of salvation still more those whom He had already offended, so that he who was filthy grew even more filthy; for, because of those who relied upon their own prudence contrary to the Word of God, there are not others who desire to cheat the Word of its salvation, nor ought we be ashamed about preaching because the preaching of the cross is a source of laughter.

Therefore He says [v. 53–57]: "Amen. Amen. I say to you, Unless you eat the flesh of the Son of Man and drink His blood, you will have no life in yourselves. He who eats My flesh and drinks My blood has eternal life, and I shall raise Him on the last day, for My flesh is truly food and My blood is truly drink. He who eats My flesh and drinks My blood remains in Me and I in him, just as the living Father (who is the source of life) has sent Me; and I live because of the Father (that is, because the Father is living in Me), so also He who eats Me himself will live also because of Me (that is, because I am in him)."

You are seeing here described the same eternal life and resurrection about which He spoke earlier so that you do not doubt the same faith in the incarnate Christ. The eating of this flesh of Christ and the drinking of this blood of Christ signifies this faith— something which we have said earlier. You see, what else can this warning: "Unless you eat the bread of the Son of Man and drink His blood, you will not have life in yourselves," mean except: "He who does not believe in Christ will be damned."?

But, that you may see that these words have the same meaning as the preceding ones, He Himself, after mentioning the eating of His flesh and the drinking of His blood, explains Himself and says [v. 58]: "This is that bread which comes down from heaven, not just as your fathers ate your manna and died, for he who eats this bread will live forever."

After these words, He said to them as they muttered [v. 61]: "Does what I have said to you offend you? What then if you will have seen the Son of Man ascending to where He was before?" This is as if He is saying: "If these words which I am preaching upon the earth offend you, although you nevertheless should believe also because of the works which I am doing, you will be offended all the more when you will have seen the Son of Man ascending to where He was before, that is, when the Son of Man Himself, who is now despised and has been preached to you, will after His glorification reign in the glory of His Father from whom He will have received power in heaven and on earth, just as He had power and glory with the Father before He descended, that is, before His incarnation. Certainly you will hear with great offense that He whom you saw crucified and dead rules over you as God over all things, if you cannot believe Him now as He performs His miracles."

Not even Christ by speaking now can separate the different natures of His divinity and humanity which are united within Him to such an extent that He may say that the very Son of Man, namely, Himself, as He passes over the earth, was in the glory of His Father in the heavens even before His incarnation. For the very Son of Man clearly is that Son of God who created all the visible and invisible things, for the Word was made flesh, something which no one denies except the spirit of the Antichrist. We say that to deny and to obscure with imagined phrases requiring explanation are the same thing. John speaks in this way [3:13]: "No one ascends into heaven except the One who comes down from heaven, the Son of Man, who is in heaven."

We mentioned earlier the things which pertain to this. This is the way we are in the habit of interpreting John 6 about faith in the incarnate Son of God. By this faith we are incorporated into Christ and Christ into us for eternal life. We receive this interpretation not from the commentaries of men, nor from our own thinking, but from the clear words of Christ interpreting Himself as you have heard.

It therefore happens that we are not interpreting these words as a reference to that external Sacrament of the body and blood of Christ, because not only does Christ not appear to be speaking about this here, but also because some words do not seem to agree with the institution of the Lord's Supper, as is apparent. Here, you see, we must always eat and drink without interruption unless we need not always believe in Christ. There, He says: "As often as you eat this bread and drink this cup of the Lord, etc.," just as Christ also says: "Do this as often as you drink, etc."

Also, here [John 6] no one eats and drinks unworthily, but all eat and drink eternal life, because faith is that eating and drinking. There, many eat and drink unworthily as they eat and drink damnation for themselves because they don't discern the body of the Lord. Although faith knows that what Christ says is there *is* there, namely, the bread as His body and the cup as His blood; nevertheless, it is the external Sacrament of which those are unworthy who abuse it in our company, not discerning the body of the Lord, although they hear "is" in the words of Christ. Also, they are not examining themselves as Christ says: "The hand of him who is betraying Me is with Me at the table."

Furthermore, here faith is taught in the flesh and blood of Christ. There we have an exercise of faith, namely, a commemoration, that is, an announcement of the Lord's death because this body which we eat in the Sacrament was offered for us and the blood which we drink was shed on the cross for the forgiveness of our sins so that because of the remembrance and endless preaching both publicly and privately which endures among us we are not permitted to accept another teaching which teaches something else which is necessary for righteousness than that Christ was given for us. That's what happened in the papacy when the true use of this Sacrament was taken away from us and for which it substituted so many abominations of Masses contrary to the institution of Christ.

Briefly, nothing is said here about the bread and wine. In fact, Christ denies that He is speaking about some external bread and cup; otherwise, the Capernaites would have taken His words more moderately, had they seen that a supper was prepared in which bread and wine were served, for, as you see, this is what they were seeking with all their heart. But who denies that there are bread and wine in the Supper which Christ instituted? There bread is broken and bread is commanded to be eaten and is eaten, and a cup is served and ordered to be drunk and is drunk. About the former, He declares: "This is My body," and about the latter: "This is My blood. Do this as often as you may have done it in remembrance of Me."

In John 6 you do not hear this. On what basis, then, would you prove that the same things are being described? You indeed hear "bread," but it is the bread which came down from heaven and not that which is broken in our hands and eaten physically. Lest along with the Capernaites you think something else, this spiritual bread is the flesh of Christ. He says: "The bread which I am giving you is My flesh." Therefore, you now have the reason why we do not interpret John 6 about that Last Supper which Christ instituted.

Some of the Sacramentarians—however, against their own conscience—seek a pretense against us under this occasion, for they suppose in this way: "The whole world understands that John 6 speaks about the Sacrament of the Supper. We shall also say that there Christ is teaching that final institution of His. Also, we shall persuade people that the faculty of Wittenberg is fleeing the light, for they deny that John 6 is speaking about a sacramental eating." You see, they think that there some things are being said clearly by which one can prove that the bread of the Supper is not the body of Christ and that the cup is not His blood. But from what source will they prove this unless first from their simple conversion and then from their accidental conversion? This is as if corrupting Scripture is the same as interpreting it!

Therefore, because they seek such a pretense against us not that they may say something in a godly way but that they may deny the word of Christ: "This is My body" and: "This is My blood," I shall now tell briefly how nothing offends us and how nothing is contrary to us and therefore how it happens in our favor if, when we interpret John 6 not as a reference to an external Supper (for we ought to teach frankly what we know), there is someone who interprets this as a reference to an external Supper. After all, we are very certain that because of this interpretation no one will be able to deny that the bread in the Supper is the body of Christ and the cup His blood, just as the ancient teachers were not at all fearful if someone denied that the bread of the Lord is the flesh of Christ and the cup His blood when they interpreted some words in John 6 as a reference to the Eucharist. In fact, they often claimed that on this basis.

First, we teach that we are to receive the body and blood of Christ in the bread and cup as often as we come together for this in Church or in our gathering with that faith with which Christ wants us to eat and drink His flesh and blood outside the Sacrament of the Eucharist, that is, with that faith by which we are incorporated into Him. This faith He teaches in John 6 and therefore everywhere in Scripture where it speaks about the righteousness which is Christ so that you see that we are not excluding John 6 from the Lord's Supper, although we do say that nothing there seems to speak to us about sacramental eating.

Therefore they have spoken about a dual eating of the body of Christ. The one is sacramental by which both the worthy and the unworthy eat, but the latter to their damnation; the other is spiritual by which only the worthy eat, for this latter is trust in Christ which the unworthy do not have, for if it is present, it makes them worthy and at the same time removes all sins. Without this faith (that is, trust in Christ), it is impossible to please God, the external Sacraments of Christ become prejudicial, the preaching of the Gospel is of no benefit to you, Christ Himself and the whole Trinity therefore are not food nor drink, and no created thing is holy for you. In the meantime, however, all those things are holy and good for believers nor are the divine things which God has created or ordained not that which they are because of our malicious abuse.

Christ Himself requires with clear words in His institution that you eat His body and blood in the Lord's Supper with this faith which He teaches in John 6. He does not only say:"This is My body" and: "This is My blood," which not even those who receive them unworthily doubt are true, and therefore for them the things which they believe are here because of the word of Christ are truly here, for I am not speaking here about the denying Sacramentarians. He also adds: "…which is given or broken for you," and: "…which is shed for you for the remission of sins." These words make quite clear with what trust Christ wants them to receive His body and blood in the Sacrament, for outside the Sacrament we cannot accept them without this trust. Moreover, in the Sacrament they can indeed be received but to damnation, so that you become guilty of the body and blood of the Lord, for you are not receiving that which Christ wants you to accept by this faith.

Next, as I have said before, we do not disapprove of the fact that some people take these statements as a reference to the external Sacrament, provided that in the meantime they speak in a godly way and have no desire to deny the truth of this interpretation of theirs which we describe elsewhere, as I now see is happening through those who say that we eat Christ by faith; therefore, we do not eat His body in the bread nor drink His blood in the cup as if we cannot eat Him in the bread by faith according to His word, or as if those who deny the word or institution of Christ have great faith.

The ancient teachers have said in their commentaries on John 6 that which they ought to have said about the spiritual eating of Christ, just as Augustine says there: "Why are you preparing your stomach and teeth? Believe, and you have eaten." In the meantime, they have also spoken about the sacramental eating which Christ instituted in the Last Supper that it not only happens through the occasion but also that they have thought that some of the words of Christ there speak about the Last Supper, because they were taking those words as a prophecy and promise of the Lord as if He promised at Capernaum that He was going to institute that external Sacrament. They also were taking those words: "The bread which I shall give you is My flesh" as: "…I shall give for the life of the world."

As you have heard, we interpret this, as the context urges, as a reference to spiritual eating by which faith we eat Christ, the bread of life which comes down from heaven, for He Himself is the heavenly bread. As He says, first, He gave His flesh, offering the Father a sacrifice in the fragrance of sweetness on the cross for the sins of the whole world. Next, He gives us that same flesh or His humanity in which God is present through the preaching of His Gospel. Those who believe in that Gospel are incorporated into Christ.

Those [Sacramentarians] or some of them have interpreted that as if Christ were promising that at some time He was going to give the Sacrament of the Eucharist. From there, they kept advancing to interpret also the rest of the words as a reference to the eating of His flesh and drinking of His blood in the same way, namely, to the eating of the visible broken bread and drinking of the external cup which Christ instituted in the Supper. They nevertheless were not teaching nor writing those heretical statements: "The bread is not the body of Christ," something which the Sacramentarians now are doing, or: "The cup or blood of Christ is not to be given to the laity," something which the papists are doing but not the sacred teachers.

Certainly the godly person will not deny that those ancients spoke piously about this subject although they said some things out of place, as it seems. I am now speaking solely about those things which they say about spiritual and sacramental eating. However, it seems to get in the way of their interpretation that the discussion of the eating and drinking in the Supper and that described in John 6 are not the same, because in the former some eat and drink damnation and become guilty of the body and blood of Christ. In the latter, whoever eats and drinks, eats and drinks not damnation but eternal life, and judgment and damnation are only for those who depart as despisers who are unwilling to eat and drink.

In this area, however, I am so far from resisting those who speak piously that I desire them also to deliberate on some appropriate interpretation. Moreover, I introduce such an interpretation for them, namely: all who eat the body of Christ and drink His blood in the Sacrament just as Christ instituted, eat and drink eternal life, and none of them eats or drinks judgment or damnation. I say they eat and drink *just as Christ instituted*, and not differently. Furthermore, He instituted that we eat by faith and not teach unfaithfully or perversely or live shamefully, as I said earlier. He also instituted the Supper for us and not against us. He says: "...which is broken *for you.*" Therefore, the same eternal life which is instituted for eating in the Supper is also taught in John 6, so that there is no need here to be offended by the interpretation of the ancients. You see, we are saying here against our Sacramentarians that here those who eat the body and drink the blood of Christ worthily are entering into the new covenant, that is, the remission of sins and eternal life. Otherwise, what Paul says would not be true, namely, that those who eat and drink unworthily are eating and drinking damnation.

Furthermore, that some people eat the Lord's body and drink His blood unworthily in the Sacrament and thus become guilty of the Lord's body and blood happens from the fact that they do indeed eat and drink that which Christ instituted; namely, the Lord's body and blood. After all, when we gather together in our congregation, the institution of Christ is not a lie because of their malice. He does not say: "If a good person comes, the bread is My body and the cup is My blood, but not if a wicked person comes." Rather, they are not eating and drinking the Lord's body and blood as Christ instituted for us to eat and drink them, as I have said. And this is not to mention now the commemoration or announcement of Christ's death which He Himself certainly did not want to be hypocritical.

"But," you say, "when they eat to their damnation the body of Christ, how in their case is it true what Christ says: '…which was broken for you'? For it seems that it is not broken *for* them but *against* them?" I respond. Just as "This is My body" is true if someone should eat unworthily, so also "…which is broken for you" is true. After all, this is the word of Christ, even if someone should receive it against himself and not for himself contrary to Christ's institution, and not discern the Lord's body nor examine himself. It is not fitting that Christ institute something or give something to us which acts against us as far as He Himself is concerned. However, if we should accept badly something which is good (that is, differently from the way He instituted it), the fault is ours and not of the giver nor of the thing given. Those are subject to a greater condemnation who either deny with their teaching this institution, as do the Sacramentarians, or who teach an abuse so that what Christ instituted does not take place, as those now do after the truth has been revealed, namely, the Mass-peddlers and forbidders of the other kind, as they are called.

I could present very many more likeness of this thing, were the matter so well-known of itself and had the ancients not treated it often; namely, that the body of Christ is not evil or that it is not in the bread because a wicked person receives it in a wicked way. Nevertheless, I shall tell one similar situation for the sake of those who are contending about the present breaking that they cannot understand the word of Christ: "...which is broken for you." If we must take this to mean the present breaking, Christ would not have said: "...is broken on your behalf." He would rather have said: "...which is broken as far as you are concerned."[9] Admirable, but I am no admirer of blindness!

In the meantime, I thank Christ for breaking or distributing His body not only for us but also on our behalf so that we have no doubt but that we are receiving eternal life. If we receive this Sacrament just as He gives it to us, it is on our behalf and not against us. If we receive it differently, He Himself indeed has given or has broken it for us, but we do not receive it on our own behalf, namely, because we have been disposed against the procedure for our salvation so that it rather was necessary for us to abstain from the Sacrament.

I therefore have heard something similar. Some good and truly friendly man invited the Pomeranian to dinner with many other friendly and pleasant dining companions. We sat at the table. The host who invited us set the foods and good wine before all the diners, among whom the Pomeranian was included, to drink therefrom and be happy and that the wine might be beneficial to those before whom it was placed that they themselves might drink. He did not do this that others who were not invited benefit from the wine. It was not poison, but good wine. The host was a good man, the wine was good, the reason for serving it was good. The guests

---

9 The Latin here is "*pro vobis* - i. e., on your behalf" and the dative of reference "*vobis.*, i. e., as concerns you," or even as an indirect object "for you."

drank and became happy. Although the Pomeranian attended this good banquet, he had to abstain from the wine not because it was bad wine or was served for an evil reason, but because I was unable to receive it well, that is, I could not receive on behalf of myself that which the host was serving me on behalf of myself and which the others did receive for themselves. This was not the fault of the giving host nor of the thing given, but my stomach was so disposed that the wine not only was not good for it but even harmed it.

With this convenient interpretation, thus we come to the aid of those who understood many things in John 6 as references to the Sacrament of the Eucharist, notwithstanding the fact that some receive the Sacrament to their judgment, because Christ teaches in John 6 the sort of eating which grants to all who eat eternal life. We also are saying that all who eat the Sacrament eat eternal life, provided they eat just as Christ instituted that we should eat it.

However, I shall also add another suitable interpretation no less forceful for the way of thinking of the ancients, and, along with our preceding one, appropriate that we may say that all who eat and drink in faith eat and drink this Sacrament for their salvation, just as all who eat and drink as Christ teaches in John 6 eat and drink eternal life. For, although even the unworthy eat the body of Christ, as Paul says, Christ considered only those as eating and drinking who are incorporated into Him by that eating. This is just as Christ considered only that woman who was laboring under that flow of blood for touching Him but not the rest of the crowd. He also stopped that flow so that no one should doubt that He was touched in such a way when she, without anyone knowing, touched very gently just His robe. Nevertheless Christ said that she touched Him with a great announcement of her faith, but He denied that the crowd touched Him. (Read this in Mark 5 and Luke 8.)

Thus Christ considers those as true eaters who not only eat the body of Christ sacramentally but at the same time also spiritually, that is, with trust in the death and blood of Christ by which faith we teach we must eat and as we do not teach, just as envy lies about us, that only external eating takes away sins. Otherwise, why is it that we say with Paul that some eat their own judgment and damnation?

Next, just as you cannot speak in that way unless you be a Manichean, that is, that Christ denies that those who did not touch Him in faith touched Him; therefore they did not touch Him, or they did not touch the true body of Christ. For among those who are eating the true body of Christ, there must be present here those who believe that the word of Christ is true: "This is My body," even if they have no trust in Christ, which is truly the Christian faith which justifies the wicked person, as we said earlier. Those do not trust Christ who embrace the sects of destruction against the doctrine of righteousness and godliness or themselves live shamefully without repenting, just as you see that those things were happening among the Corinthians.

From these, each person can see that we are not resisting the ancients who interpreted John 6 as a reference to the Eucharist, nor are we now wrestling against those who want to interpret it in that way, lest that spiritual malice (that is, that wickedness which boasts against our carnality), imagines that we here are fleeing some light and says: "The Wittenbergians do not interpret John 6 as a reference to the Sacrament. They see that there those things are said through which one can prove that the bread of the Supper is the body of Christ." It is a lie that we cannot prove it from there, even if you turn around and upside down all the words and corrupt their whole way of thinking, as I showed earlier about those who boast that we must take all the words of Christ's institution in their primary and proper meaning. Nevertheless this does not cause the bread in the Supper not to be the body of Christ nor the cup not to be the blood for those who eat and drink there. After all, no matter in what direction they turn, we are not so blind (by the grace of Christ) that we do not see what the words of Christ and what their words are, and what Christ says and what they themselves are corrupting. We retain the words of Christ and their sense.

However, we send back to Satan (the master of error) those strange and spirituous corruptions and changes as well as those human additions. Now, as always, he causes trouble for the Gospel of Christ, but he will not prevail. Only those perish who should perish. The mercy of Christ will lead back to us from their error the rest in an appropriate manner at the proper time. It is close to the time that Satan, who has already been judged, be judged. Amen.

Therefore I indeed do not want to defend this interpretation by which they interpret John 6 as a reference to the Eucharist, for you have seen above what I perceive from the manifest words of Christ and from the context. Nevertheless, I am pleased rather to do too much, as you have seen, by coming to the aid of the ancients than to yield to this wicked calumny. You see, if you accept John 6 as a reference to the Eucharist, the meaning will hold firm for no one rather than for those who confess from the words of Christ that the bread in the Supper is the body of Christ, and these words will clearly be the same, namely: "The bread is My body," and: "The bread which I shall give is My flesh which I shall give for the life of the world." Also, if you go on to ask of what benefit that flesh is, you hear: "My flesh truly is food, and My blood truly is drink. He who eats, etc."

Therefore, whether they have read the words of the institution of Christ in their own order, or whether they have changed and perverted them all, they will not prove from John 6 or from the words which were once written on John 6—I say, they will not prove that in the Supper the bread of Christ is not the body of Christ or that the cup is not the blood of Christ. Also, they will not only be subverters of the words of the institution of Christ when, because of these words: "My flesh is truly food," they change those words: "The bread is My body" and say: "My body is bread" with that spirituous tail "is bread," to wit, spiritual bread. But, even after subverting and inverting the words of the Supper, they will be compelled by the same logic which you perhaps may call "a strange conversion" through contrapositioning or through impossibility, if such a thing ever happened, to read these words of John 6: "The bread which I shall give is My flesh, which I shall give for the life of the world," so that everywhere they are converters and corrupters. They certainly turn around the words of the cup through the impossible, as you heard earlier. These things must happen to those who oppose their opinions and the thoughts of human hearts to the clear word of Christ.

But someone of our friends says here: "Because you were unwilling to resist those who interpret John 6 as a reference to the Eucharist, despite the fact that you understand and teach otherwise, but because you preferred quite cleverly to be present with a convenient interpretation for this reason alone—that you not offer a handle for a calumny, etc.—how will that threat of Christ stand firm if someone take it as a reference to the Eucharist: 'Unless you eat the flesh of the Son of Man and drink His blood, you will not have life within yourselves'? For this warning will appear similar to that other one: 'Unless a person be born again of water and the Spirit, he will not be able to enter the kingdom of God'; and thus no one will be saved unless he eat the body of Christ in the Sacrament and drink His blood."

I respond. I believe that this is true about those who hold this Sacrament in contempt and never receive it, but not about those who cannot receive it because of their age or because of an illness or because it is denied them among the papists, or because they are in prison, or because they are living among unbelievers or Turks or others, etc. For it is not the latter but the former who despise the institution and word of Christ, who says: "Do this, etc.; as often as you drink, etc." These words truly do not permit you to despise this Sacrament so that you never come when it can be given to you according to the institution of Christ. After all: "Do this" does not means: "Despise, etc." And: "…as often as you eat" does not mean: "You will never eat."

Listen, therefore, if you will permit here an appropriate interpretation. The faithful always eat the flesh and drink the blood of Christ spiritually so long as they have believed in Christ, as we have said on the basis of John 6. Of the number of these are those who cannot receive in the congregation of the faithful, even in the external Sacrament, the body and blood of Christ. They nevertheless do receive the same Sacrament in their prayerful desire, for they wished to receive it gladly so that it is not against them even if you take "Unless you have eaten, etc." as a reference to the Sacrament. This, you see, is the prayer and desire of those who cannot receive the Sacrament. All the more does this please Christ than the eating of those who do not have this desire, for the latter eat judgment as they eat, while the former eat eternal life, even when they do not eat.

I am not saying new things now, but they have spoken in this way even before us. Why are we not saying this about the Sacrament of the Eucharist when we assert that that person who has even been born again of water and the Spirit, who believes in Christ, wishes with the greatest desire the Baptism of water but cannot receive it before he dies? After all, who will doubt that such a case can occur, as being held in prison among unbelievers?

"But," you say, "our little children do not have this desire to eat and drink; therefore they do not eat and drink. If they do not eat and drink physically, because we do not give them anything, neither do they eat and drink spiritually. Because they have no such desire, they do not have life in themselves but are condemned."

I respond that I have my hands full with the persons which I have taken up here to say that the statement of Christ: "Unless you will have eaten, etc." can be understood among those who accept this as said with reference to the Eucharist to mean those who must and can receive the Sacrament, among whom, as I shall say below, are not our little children. After all, we must not seek this from John 6, where this is not said even in disguise. Rather, we must seek it from the institution of the Last Supper, which in my judgment does not admit little children, as I shall say later.

We indeed must baptize our little children that they may accept this covenant of God, just as the infants of the Jews received circumcision. Our little children have been born and can be born again of water and the Holy Spirit, as Christ says: "Permit the little children to come to Me, for of such, that is, of little children who are offered to Me, is the kingdom of heaven." Furthermore, in my judgment, we ought not give the Eucharist to them. Nevertheless, they do not go without the flesh and blood of Christ or without Christ Himself, because, as we read in Rom. 6[:3]: "For as many of us as have been baptized into Christ have been baptized into His death"; Gal. 3[:27]: "As many of you as have been baptized have put on Christ"; and Eph. 5[:25–26]: "Christ loved the Church (in which undoubtedly are our infants unless you should say they belong to Satan) and gave Himself for her to sanctify her with the washing of water in the Word, etc.," that we may be members of the body of Christ of His flesh and bones.

We have now attended sufficiently—and more!—to the interpreters of John 6 regarding the Eucharist, although, as you have seen earlier, we do not interpret that as a reference to the Eucharist. I say this so that our adversaries not imagine that we are fleeing the light, despite the fact that I don't see how we would flee the light. Furthermore, because a person fears some peril from that way of thinking which we judge is not native to John 6, all the authority of all the ancient teachers should grant that a different interpretation is not the confirmation of any error. When something is said piously, why should it not be pleasing, however much it is out of place? But when some error is confirmed as a result of this, human authority must fall, however great it may be, so that the truth of God may stand firm.

Here there is the danger if, because of a different interpretation regarding the Eucharist which one can hold secondarily, what is native and real be denied. This is true if that interpretation is different from what the context requires and what Christ expressed in very clear language. Next, I feel that we must not endure the danger that, because of this interpretation, we are compelled to give our infants the body and blood of Christ. For where Christ threatens in this way: "Unless you will have eaten, etc.," no appropriate interpretation will deliver our conscience in so serious a matter.

On the contrary, in fact, let us give our little ones that from which they may have life, just as at the time of Cyprian they formerly used to give infants the Eucharist not just once after Baptism but often in the Church. Augustine, too, compelled as he was from this passage of John, judges that no one should hope for any salvation or eternal life without Baptism and without the body and blood of the Lord. He also judged that without these we promise life and salvation to our infants in vain, something which you can read in Augustine, *de peccatorum meritis et remissione*, Bk. 1, c. 24. Why would they do that? They were understanding these words [from John] as a reference to the Eucharist. As a result, the need to give children the Sacrament followed.

Therefore, it remains to seek through God the simplest interpretation of Scripture in all matters, even if some different interpretation should offer itself in the meantime to be accepted in one way or another, especially in those passages which deal with faith and those which are necessary for salvation. There we rarely become involved in a sense different from the very words without danger.

The Bohemians today are also said to give the Sacrament to their infants. Also, the fact that in many churches of Germany children who have already received Baptism receive an ablution, as they call it, before the altar, seems to be a vestige of the custom among us that children formerly were brought to the altar where they were communed with the body and blood of Christ. It seems that, after the abolition of such a communion, the common folk were not really satisfied to agree with this.

The minister who officiates at a Mass offers peace to the bystanders in those Masses, that is, he presses to their mouth or offers for their kiss that which they call "the peace," that is, some small image or gold or silver cross. That is a vestige of that ancient practice which you see in Cyprian, sermon 5, "On The Lapsed," when the deacon offered those who were present the body of the Lord and the sacred cup of Christ, a reality which now not only has been lost but even forbidden by the papists and condemned. We show the common folk the hypocrisy of images and of precious stones and of gold and silver and press that against their mouth lest they receive nothing from the altar. They certainly keep nothing for themselves and bring everything back to the altar. This, I say, is a very certain argument of the fact that we still retain that ancient title among ourselves, for we call this "giving the peace," something which used to mean at the time of Cyprian that we are not offering gold and silver to be kissed, as now, but to admit one to the communion of the body and blood of Christ, something which you often see in Cyprian, especially in Epistle 2, Bk. 1. But I say these things in passing.

On the basis of the institution of Christ, I judge with certainty that it is not necessary that we give the Eucharist to little children, something which nevertheless Christian teachers did as necessary in the time of Cyprian, two hundred years after the glorification of Christ, and even later at the time of Augustine. Also, Augustine himself along with others declared that it was necessary from the words of Christ: "Unless you have eaten, etc."

After all, Christ instituted this Sacrament in remembrance of Himself, but infants cannot commemorate nor announce the death of the Lord. Also, according to Paul, they cannot discern the body of the Lord. What Paul says, therefore, does not befit them: "Moreover, a person should examine Himself and thus eat of that bread and drink of that cup." [1 Cor. 11:28]

Now there are those who, contrary to the clear ordinations of God and the expressed words of Christ, are in the habit of wickedly foisting upon us a prescription of a long time and of crying out: "The fathers, the fathers, the fathers!" It is not enough for them that we confess the Christian, Catholic, and Apostolic Church, unless they also make for us the Cyprian, Augustinian, Gregorian, etc. churches. When did Christ ever give us a command about Cyprian or Augustine or others? When they preach the Gospel which Christ commanded the apostles to preach, we must listen to them; but when, as men, they teach their own material without Scripture or create new articles of faith from poorly-understood Scripture which we have to accept, we must resist them and not accept them according to that command: "Examine all things, and hold onto what is good." [I The. 5:21]

They themselves (as also we) should build not upon themselves but, as we read in Eph. [2:20], "upon the foundation of the prophets and apostles, Jesus Christ Himself, being the cornerstone"; but this foundation of the prophets and apostles is the same as what they themselves presented in their teaching, which is Jesus Christ (1 Cor. 3[:11]).

Here each teacher or preacher of the Church until the end of the world (even Cyprian, even Augustine, etc.) should see how he builds upon [the foundation] that he teach the sort of things which are necessary and not perish when the truth has been revealed and the day and fire come. Only the word of the Lord will stand firm forever. These things, however, are not of Christ's institution.

What will our adversaries have with which to cover up this error of the holy martyrs and teachers by which they have said on the basis of these words: "Unless you will have eaten, etc.," that infants cannot have life unless they receive the Eucharist? You see, if they may have said that they didn't err, they will condemn themselves for not giving infants today the Sacrament, as they neglect their eternal life, and will condemn our infants who will die without having received the Eucharist. But if they may have said that they did make a mistake, contrary to truth already revealed from the Word of God, let them stop throwing up to us a prescription of long duration and the authority of the fathers. Rather, let them follow along with us the authority of God the Father of our Lord Jesus Christ and of the holy apostles that they may be along with us in the one Catholic and Apostolic Church.

However I am not at that point of condemning those who today still give the Sacrament to infants as if it be a sin to give it, for I have no command to do this and that I, too, not err when I correct the error of others. I also must see to it how I build upon Christ the Foundation, lest I make a necessity of not giving it just as the ancients made a necessity of giving it. I dare not forbid what they commanded badly.

After all, someone could defend that this is a free matter and say: "Although infants do not commemorate nor announce the death of Christ, although they do not discern the body of Christ, nevertheless they are in this congregation and belong to this congregation in which we do have this commemoration and in which we do discern the body of Christ which they are unable to do and should not do but which others do to whom the infants themselves do belong. Also, that does not seem to be against the command: 'Moreover, let a person examine himself, etc.,' because infants who have received Baptism and whom the Holy Spirit has sanctified, that is, whom Christ has accepted because they were offered to

Him, do not have anything to examine, that is, anything which displeases Christ, because He says: 'Of such is the kingdom of heaven.'"

To give such infants the Sacrament, therefore, perhaps may be permitted, but to make out of the words of Christ which have not been sufficiently understood: "Unless you will have eaten, etc." the necessity to give them the Sacrament without which they cannot receive salvation ought not be something that the Christian preacher or teacher of the Church wants to have against himself.

In the meantime, I have been saying all these things freely about John 6 both that I might disclose our way of thinking about it and that I might also take away the opportunity from those who seek therefrom an opportunity for denying that the bread of the Lord in the Supper is His body and the cup His blood and who, if they have said that in this chapter Christ is speaking about the Sacrament of the bread and wine, are doing this at their peril. They will accomplish nothing against the words of Christ: "This is My body" and: "This is My blood." As I have said, the changes of some are laughable.

Moreover, if they may have said that Christ is speaking here about spiritual eating which we call faith in the incarnate Son of God by which we are incorporated into Him, they will have no conflict with us. Next, if they may have said that John 6 concerns only spiritual eating and that in the Supper there is only a spiritual eating of the body and blood of Christ, they will not prove that nor will they establish that consequence until they have not taken away from the Supper the bread about which Christ declares: "This is My body" and the cup about which Christ also declares here: "This is My blood."

Through these pages, therefore, I want to be of service to those who are opposed to the sacred institution of Christ, especially to those changers or inverters of the words of Christ who before earnestly entreated us both in their private writings and in their words in our presence, but who now have asked us in their public writing for our response. But, if they do not listen, God will find those to whom not only these things which I have written about John 6 but also all things which I have written earlier about the Sacrament are beneficial. They will be able to bring false charges against my words, a trick which they know well, that they may force into my hands a strange book in an ignorant, shameless, and wicked way. However, they will never be able to establish their dreams, changes, and additions against the institution of the Lord's Supper because: "Heaven and earth may pass away, but the word of Christ will endure forever." [Mat. 24:35]

God knows what I perceive about the bread and cup of the Lord. Let all that I have now written be my testimony before all people. Amen.

Set in type by Johann Luft
1528 A.D.